D0149203

Composition Practice Book 2

Second Edition

A Text for English Language Learners

Linda Lonon Blanton

University of New Orleans
New Orleans, Louisiana

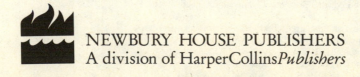

NEWBURY HOUSE PUBLISHERS
A division of HarperCollins*Publishers*

Director: Laurie E. Likoff
Text and Cover Design: Suzanne Bennett Associates
Text Illustration: Kathie Kelleher
Production Coordinator: Cynthia Funkhouser
Compositor: Crane Typesetting Service, Inc.
Printer and Binder: Malloy Lithographing, Inc.

ISBN: 0-06-632052-6

NEWBURY HOUSE PUBLISHERS
A division of HarperCollins*Publishers*

Language Science
Language Teaching
Language Learning

Composition Practice, Book 2, Second Edition

Library of Congress Cataloging in Publication Data

Blanton, Linda Lonon, 1942–
  Composition practice.
  Second ed. of: Elementary composition practice. c1978–
1979.
  1. English language—Textbooks for foreign speakers.
2. English language—Composition and exercises.
I. Blanton, Linda Lonon, 1942–   Elementary
composition practice.   II. Title.
PE1128.B588   1989   808'.042   88-17976

92 91 90   9 8 7 6 5

Preface

Composition Practice: Book 2 grew out of materials developed for an intensive reading and composition course for adult learners of English as a second language. Book 2 is a composition text designed for students on a high-elementary or low-intermediate level, although it is realized that the terms *elementary* and *intermediate* may vary from program to program. *Composition Practice: Book 1*, the lead book in the series, is considered to be the first composition book adults learning English would work through; Book 2 follows, expands, and reinforces the lessons contained in Book 1.

The materials contained in *Composition Practice: Book 2* are not self-instructional; they presume the presence of a professional teacher. A section following the Contents, entitled ''To the Teacher,'' gives suggestions as to how the materials can be used effectively. Anyone using or contemplating use of the materials is urged to read that section.

Composition Practice: Book 2 is divided into ten units. Each unit contains an illustrated reading passage, followed by exercises on comprehension, grammar, vocabulary, textual cohesion, order, or writing mechanics. Notes and questions on the organization of the reading passage, designed to help the teacher guide students in discussion, lead into a model composition, which makes use of the vocabulary, grammatical structures, and organizational framework of the reading passage. Students are then presented with detailed instructions for writing their own compositions. All reading passages and model compositions focus on certain kinds of composition writing, such as narration and description, and certain patterns of organization, such as chronological order, spatial order, and classification.

The assumption behind these materials is that there is more to writing on even an elementary level than unconnected sentence exercises. It is felt that beginning students can understand and practice sophisticated principles and techniques of English composition writing without waiting until they know more English. The strict criterion is that these techniques and principles be presented simply and methodically. It is felt that both Book 1 and Book 2 adhere to that criterion.

I wish to thank ESL/EFL colleagues, both local and worldwide, who have responded with support and valuable criticism to *Composition Practice: Book 1* and with encouragement for the continuation of the series. Their attention is greatly appreciated.

Contents

To the Teacher

The materials in *Composition Practice, Books 1 and 2*, are based on the presupposition that beginning level English language students can indeed write compositions, not just do writing-type exercises, as long as they are allowed, in preparation for writing their compositions, to become familiar with organizational and situational frameworks and are supplied with vocabulary and grammatical structures to use within those frameworks. The methodology involves creating an awareness of different modes of organization which lend themselves to the ordering of different kinds of data in English. For example, details of a person's daily life lend themselves well to chronological ordering. In addition, students must learn the structure vocabulary, i.e., vocabulary for expressing relationships, which the language provides for ordering within a particular organizational framework. For example, data ordered chronologically can be tied together with *first*, *next*, *afterwards*, etc. It is assumed that this approach will make students better writers and readers, for data in the new language will no longer appear in a formless mass.

Composition Practice: Book 2 is designed for students of English as a second language of high elementary or low intermediate levels of proficiency. It is intended for adults who want to learn English for professional, academic, and business reasons. The format, as well as some of the actual lessons, have been tested successfully with students ranging in age from 15 to 55, from nine different language backgrounds and of educational backgrounds ranging from ninth grade to university degrees. The text provides 40 to 50 class hours of instruction (an intensive 8- to 10-week course).

Book 2 is divided into ten units, each containing an illustrated reading passage, exercises on the reading, a model composition, and instructions for the student's composition. The instructions accompanying each exercise are written as simply as possible, yet in some cases may need further oral explanation. The notes and questions on the organization of each preceding reading passage, to be found at the end of the exercise section in each unit, are intended for the teacher's use in guiding students, in oral discussion, toward a conscious understanding of the functional nature of paragraphing (to introduce the topic, to discuss the topic, to conclude the topic) and the ordering of information within those paragraphs (chronological order, spatial order, classification, etc.).

The readings, each with a companion model set within the same organizational and situational framework, progress in grammatical difficulty along the following lines: they move from the simple present tense to the present continuous tense, from the future with **be going to** to the simple past, and then to the present perfect, with modals interspersed along the way. This progression was chosen because the lessons in beginning grammar classes are often so ordered and it is assumed that students using *Composition Practice: Book 2* will be studying grammar separately and simultaneously. If that is not the case, the teacher can build grammatical explanations, examples, and more grammar-based exercises into each unit.

The exercises following each reading are varied for the sake of maintaining student interest, as well as covering more ground over the entire text. The notion of *cohesion* is introduced in the exercises and can be explained simply as the "glue" that holds ideas together, sometimes within sentences, sometimes across sentences. As students do the exercises on *reference* and *connection*, both of which help to provide cohesion, they will begin to understand the concept.

The model composition in each unit makes use of the grammatical structures, vocabulary, and organization of the reading passage. It is a shorter, simpler version of the reading passage and serves as the immediate resource for the student's ensuing composition. Students should not copy the model, but rather use its ideas, grammatical structures, vocabulary, etc., to create their own compositions.

An attempt was made in all reading passages and model compositions to make the content realistic by focusing on people like any of us who work and play and study. Specific places are mentioned, but the locale should be unimportant for the comprehension of the readings and students will substitute their own environments in their writing. It is felt that this personalization of the topic facilitates writing competence.

The instructions for the student's own composition at the end of each unit should be interpreted and explained by the teacher. The teacher should closely supervise to see that these instructions are understood and followed. Each entire unit is designed to prepare the student for the composition which, in a sense, culminates the unit. The purpose of what precedes each composition is to provide the student with the mind-set within which to create his own composition and the linguistic tools with which to do so. The diagram at the end of each page of "Instructions for student's composition" is there to give a visual image of the shape of the composition in terms of paragraphs. Simply drawing boxes on the blackboard and talking about what goes in each "box" is often helpful as part of a precomposition discussion. In some diagrams, the label "body" is used, while in others, it is not. Where it is not used, the conclusion of the preceding reading passage and model composition is not a separate component that follows the body. Instead, the contents are organized so that the final paragraph of the body serves as the conclusion to the composition. That dual function is something which students will understand as they work through the "Notes and questions on the organization of the reading" in each unit.

The pictures that illustrate the reading passage in each unit can be used for oral and written composition. The teacher can read the "story" while students follow the meaning in the pictures. Additional composition practice in each unit can come from having students write what they see in the pictures.

The readings and models are primarily descriptive (Units 3, 4, 9) and narrative (Units 1, 5, 7) in type. Units 2 and 6 are in letter form: Unit 2, a friendly letter, and Unit 6, a business letter. Units 8 and 10 are expository. Six different organizational frameworks are presented and are used either singly or in combination:

Chronological order (a time arrangement): Units 1, 4, 5, 7
Classification (a narrowing subject focus): Units 3, 8, 9, 10
Spatial order (a space arrangement): Unit 2
Shift of focus (from one subject to another, all tied to the speaker): Unit 2
Ranking (a hierarchical arrangement): Unit 6
Balance of contrasts (equalization of focus): Unit 9

Students should be made consciously aware of these frameworks as they progress through the materials. Diagrams are often useful for a visual grasp of the organizational concepts:

Chronological order: *Example:* 9:00, 9:30, 9:45

Classification: *Example:* the weather, divided into fall, spring, summer, winter

Spatial order: a.   b.   *Example:* left and right / first, second, and third

Shift of focus: *Example:* my place, I, you

Ranking: *Example:* biggest, average, smallest

Balance of contrasts: a.   b.   *Example:* tall/short / fat/thin

Each unit is designed to provide material for five hours of class work. If students meet for composition five days a week, in an intensive program, all of the basic work can be done in class. If they meet fewer days per week, the exercises can be assigned as homework and one unit can still be completed in a week's time.

The following is a five-day suggested breakdown of each unit:

Day 1: *Reading*

The teacher presents the context of the reading orally several times, as if telling a story. Students listen, following along with the pictures. Next, the teacher reads the text aloud, while students follow, reading silently. New words and grammatical structures are explained. Students then read silently again, using dictionaries to recheck any problem vocabulary. The teacher next asks questions about the reading which students answer by finding the sentence where the answer appears and reading it aloud. Then, the teacher writes sequential questions about the reading on the board. Students are called on to retell the text by answering the questions without reference to the book. (The teacher may want to omit some of these steps as the proficiency of the students increases.)

Day 2: *Exercises*

Students complete the exercises and go through the notes/questions on the organization of the reading passage. If there is enough time, the exercises are checked orally.

Day 3: *Presentation of Model*

If the exercises were not checked before, they are checked now. Then, the model is presented by following some or all of the steps used in presenting the reading text on Day 1. Next, the teacher goes over the instructions for the students' compositions. Drawing boxes on the blackboard to represent paragraphs and labeling them as to their function and content is often helpful. The students' homework assignment for Day 4 is to mentally plan their compositions or plan them on paper in outline or note form. (The teacher may need to show students how to make notes or an outline.)

Day 4: *Composition*

Students write their compositions in class. They should not copy the model, but exhaust the resources it provides.

Day 5: *Wrap-up*

The class should finish any work that is left over from Days 1–4. If the teacher has checked all of the compositions, common problems can be explained. Orally or with an overhead projector, compositions that illustrate points that the teacher wants to make might be shared with the class. The teacher may want students to rewrite their compositions, correcting and expanding.

Some composition classes in nonintensive programs may meet only two hours per week over a sixteen-week period. The students in such a program could take as long as two weeks to complete a unit and still cover most of the material in the book. The breakdown of each unit might then appear as follows:

Day 1 of the first week: *Reading*
The teacher presents the content of the reading according to the procedure outlined for Day 1 of the preceding five-day suggested plan for each unit. The student's homework for Day 2 is to do the exercises.

Day 2 of the first week: *Presentation of Model*
The exercises done for homework are checked orally. Then, the model is presented by following some or all of the steps used in presenting the reading text on Day 1. Next, the teacher goes over the instructions for the students' compositions. The students' homework assignment is to plan their compositions in outline or note form.

Day 1 of the second week on the unit: *Composition*
The teacher goes over the model again quickly in order to review and then the teacher checks students' notes or outlines. Students then write their compositions in class.

Day 2 of the second week on the unit: *Wrap-up*
The teacher follows the procedure outlined for Day 5 of the preceding five-day plan for each unit.

Whatever the schedule, it is desirable that the actual writing of the compositions be done in class where the teacher is present to answer questions, make corrections, and offer suggestions. Students should be instructed to keep their compositions for future reference. At the end of the school term, the teacher can prepare a table of contents for a special composition notebook that each student prepares, containing all the numbered and dated composition work for the term and including notes or outlines, original drafts, and rewrites of each composition. This notebook can serve as a handy reference for future composition work.

After working through all the materials in this text, students should be able to write a one-page descriptive, narrative, or expository composition on a familiar, everyday subject. It will have an introduction, a body, and a conclusion and be developed within the organizational framework of chronological order, classification, spatial order, shift of focus, ranking, or balance of contrasts.

To the Student

You will need the following materials:

1. a loose-leaf notebook

2. 8½ × 11 inch loose-leaf notebook paper

3. a pen and pencil

4. a good translation dictionary and a simplified English-English dictionary

You should follow these rules for good reading:

1. Look at the complete reading selection before you use your dictionary. The meaning might become clear to you.

2. Let your eyes catch groups of words; do not stop after every word.

3. Do not move your mouth when you read; read with your eyes.

4. After you read the complete selection, use your dictionary to find the words that you do not know.

5. Read the selection again; look for important connections: *and*, *because*, *after*, *before*, *while*, etc.

You should follow these rules for good writing:

1. Leave margins: left, right, top, and bottom.

2. Indent each paragraph.

3. Put a period at the end of each sentence. Put a question mark at the end of each question. Put an exclamation mark if you want to show strong emotion.

   Examples: John is absent today.
   Is he sick?
   He had a terrible day!

4. Use capital letters correctly:

   a. names of people
   Example: John Andres
   b. names of cities
   Example: Paris

c.   names of countries
Example: Japan
d.   names of rivers
Example: the Amazon River
e.   names of streets
Example: Michigan Avenue
f.   names of buildings
Example: the Empire State Building
g.   names of organizations
Example: the United Nations
h.   names of national, ethnic, and racial groups of people
Example: French, Jewish, Spanish
i.   titles
Example: Dr. Santini
j.   the first person singular pronoun: *I*
k.   days of the week
Example: Thursday
l.   months of the year
Example: July
m.   holidays
Example: Christmas
n.   titles of books, magazines, newspapers
Example: Time
o.   the first letter at the beginning of each sentence and each question
Example: Are you happy?

Placement of Parts of a Composition

Your name
Course

Title

XXXXXXXXXXXXXXXXXXXXXXXXXXXXXXXXXXXXXXXX.
XXXXXXXXXXXXXXXXXXXXXXXXXXXXXX. XXXXXXXXXXX
XXXXXXXXXXXXXXXXXXXXXXXXXXXXXXXXX. XXXXXXX
XXXXXXXXXXXXXXXXXXX. XXXXXXXXXXXXXXXXXXXXXX
XXXXXXXXXXXXXXXXXXXXXXXXXXXXX.

XXXXXXXXXXXXXXXXXXXXXXXXXXXXXXXXXX
XXXXXXXX. XXXXXXXXXXXXXXXXXXXXXXXXXXXXXXXXX
XXXXXXXXXXXXXXXXXXXXXXXXXXXXXXXXXX. XXXXX
XXXXXXXXXXXXXXXXXXXXXXXXXXXXXXXXXX
XXXXXXXXXXXXXXXXXXXXXXXX. XXXXXXXXXXXX
XXXXXXXXXXXXXXXXXXXXXXXXXXXXXXXX. XXXXXX
XXXXXXXXXXXXXXXX. XXXXXXXXXXXXXXXXXXXXXX
XXXXXXXXXXXXXXXXXXXX.

XXXXXXXXXXXXXXXXXXXXXXXXXXXXXXX.
XXXXXXXXXXXXXXXXXXXXXXXXXXXX. XXXXXXXXXX
XXXXXXXXXXXXXXXXXXXXXXXXXXXXXXXXXXXXXXXX
XXXXXXXXXXXXX. XXXXXXXXXXXXXXXXXXXXXXXXXX
XXXXXXXXXX.

left margin ←   [ ] indentation   → right margin

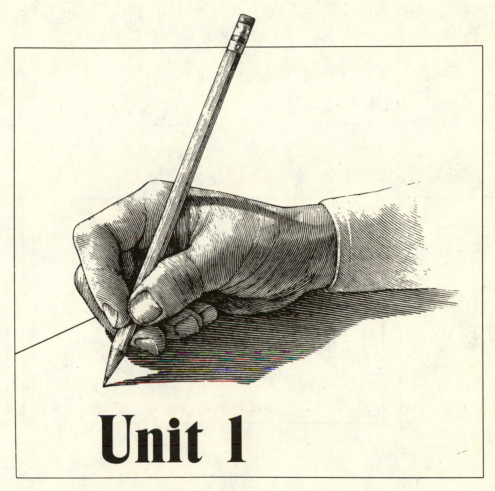

Unit 1

Composition Focus: Narration

Organizational Focus: Chronological Order

Grammatical Focus: Simple Present Tense
　　　　　　　　　　Frequency Words, e.g., *usually,*
　　　　　　　　always

1

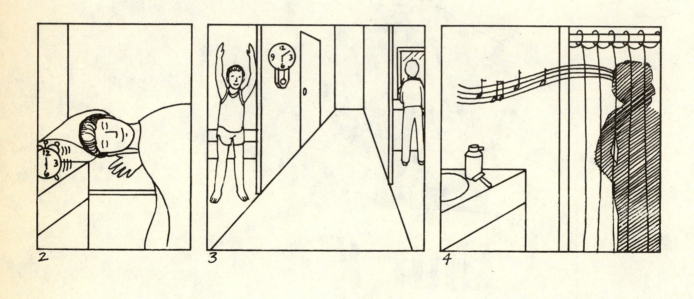

2   3   4

5

6   7

Reading 1

BRUNO'S DAILY ACTIVITIES

Bruno Baroni lives in an apartment in New Orleans. He lives with his mother, father, and older brother. The apartment is small. He shares a bedroom with his brother. Bruno is a student. He goes to school every day. He works part time in a music store after school.

Bruno gets up about 6:00 every morning. An alarm clock wakes him up. He tries to stay in shape, so he always does exercises for ten or fifteen minutes. By this time, it is his turn in the bathroom. He showers and shaves. He always gets dressed before he eats breakfast. For breakfast, he usually has coffee, toast, and fruit. He doesn't like to eat a big breakfast. After breakfast, he cleans up the kitchen while his brother reads the sports section of the newspaper. Bruno listens to the morning news on the radio while he does the dishes. By 7:30, he and his brother are ready to leave for school. They go to school by car.

Bruno and his brother, Roberto, usually arrive at school at 7:45. Roberto goes straight to class. Bruno goes to the library for about a half hour. Then, he meets his girlfriend, Maria, for a cup of coffee before class. His first class starts at 9:00. He is in class from 9:00 to 12:00. He has three classes in a row. He studies English composition, algebra, and chemistry. He works hard, but he likes his classes. After class, Bruno has lunch with Roberto and Roberto's girlfriend, Sylvia. Then, Roberto drives him to his job at the music store. Bruno works there three afternoons a week.

8

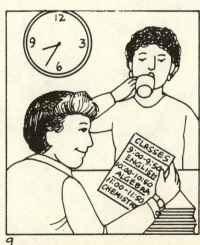
9

10

In the evening, Bruno has dinner with his family. Sometimes, he cooks dinner. He is a good cook. After dinner, he relaxes while Roberto helps with the dishes. Then, Bruno studies. He always has a lot of homework. Roberto studies, too. They study together at the kitchen table.

All in all, Bruno's days are long and tiring. He works hard and he sometimes gets discouraged. Most of the time, however, he feels good about his life.

Exercise A: Comprehension

Please circle the letter to show the correct information. The information comes from Reading 1.

1. Bruno lives in
   a. a house.
   b. an apartment.
   c. a dormitory.

2. He lives
   a. with his family.
   b. with a roommate.
   c. with his cousin.

3. He is
   a. a student.
   b. a bus driver.
   c. a carpenter.

4. He does exercises because
   a. he is very fat.
   b. he wants to stay in shape.
   c. he likes to play baseball.

5. He gets dressed
   a. before breakfast.
   b. during breakfast.
   c. after breakfast.

6. He goes to school
   a. by bus.
   b. on foot.
   c. by car.

7. After school, he works
   a. at a sporting goods store.
   b. at a grocery store.
   c. at a music store.

8. He eats dinner
   a. with his family.
   b. with a friend.
   c. alone.

9. In the evening, Bruno
   a. drinks beer.
   b. goes dancing.
   c. studies.

10. All in all, Bruno's days are
   a. full of fun.
   b. long and tiring.
   c. relaxing.

Exercise B: Simple Present Tense (3rd-Person Singular)

Please list at least ten of Bruno's daily activities. Use the *simple present tense*. Pay attention to the 3rd-person singular verb form.

Example: *He gets up at 6:00.*
                He does exercises.
                etc.

1. _____
2. _____
3. _____
4. _____
5. _____
6. _____
7. _____
8. _____
9. _____
10. _____

Exercise C: Simple Present Tense

Please rewrite "Bruno's Daily Activities" (Reading 1). Change the title to "John and Paul's Daily Activities." Be sure to indent at the beginning of each new paragraph. Make all necessary changes. Begin this way:

JOHN AND PAUL'S DAILY ACTIVITIES

> John and Paul live in an apartment in New Orleans. They live with their mother, father, and older brother. The apartment is small. They share a bedroom with their brother.

Exercise D: Frequency Words

Please rewrite the following sentences. Put the *frequency word* in parentheses into the sentence. Be careful with the word order.

    Example: Bruno does exercises after he gets up.   (always)
              Bruno always does exercises after he gets up.

1. For breakfast, he has coffee and toast.   (usually)

    _____

2. He leaves for school at 7:30.   (sometimes)

    _____

3. He goes to school by car.   (always)

    _____

4. He is on time.   (always)

    _____

5. He goes to the library before class.   (usually)

    _____

6. He cooks dinner.   (sometimes)

    _____

7. Bruno and Roberto watch TV, listen to the radio, or read.   (rarely)

    _____

8. Bruno goes to bed early.   (rarely)

    _____

9. He stays up late.   (usually)

    _____

10. Bruno has a busy day.   (usually)

    _____

Notes and Questions on the *Organization* of Reading 1

Part A: Paragraphs

Reading 1 has five paragraphs. They tell the story of Bruno's daily life. Go back to Reading 1. Be sure that you see five paragraphs. The following questions will help you understand the system of paragraphs in Reading 1:

1. Where do you find information about the beginning of Bruno's day? Which paragraph?

2. Where do you find information about Bruno's school? Which paragraph?

3. Where do you find information about Bruno's evening?

4. What information does the first paragraph give? Why is it there?

5. Look at the last paragraph. It is very short. What does *all in all* mean? Why is the last paragraph there?

Part B: Order

The word *order* refers to what is first, what is second, what is third, etc., in your composition. There should be a reason for what is first, what is second, etc. The following questions will help you understand the order of Reading 1:

1. How much time does the second paragraph cover?

2. How much time does the third paragraph cover?

3. How much time does the fourth paragraph cover?

4. Is 6:00 a.m. before or after 7:30 a.m.?

5. Is 9:00 a.m. before or after 12:00 noon?

6. Is the order in the second, third, and fourth paragraphs from early to late or from late to early?

Time order is called *chronological order*. It can go from late to early or from early to late. Think of different composition topics that might use time order.

Notice these connecting words in Reading 1:

by this time	*by* (specific time)
before	*from* (time) *to* (time)
after	*then*
while	*in the* (part of the day)

All of these words have a time meaning. Ask your teacher for more examples if you don't understand. Now, please go on to Model 1.

Model 1

MARIA'S DAILY ACTIVITIES

Maria lives in a small apartment in New Orleans. It is on the second floor of an old building. She lives with her cousin. Maria is a student at Lake College. She is studying psychology. She works part time as a clerk in a department store.

Maria gets up early every morning. She usually takes a shower and gets dressed before she has breakfast. She doesn't usually have much time for breakfast, so she has only a piece of toast and a cup of coffee. After breakfast, she quickly cleans up the kitchen. Then, she leaves for school. She always goes to school by bus.

Maria arrives at school about 8:30. First, she goes to the cafeteria to meet her boyfriend, Bruno, and have another quick cup of coffee. Then she goes to class. She is in class from 9:00 to 1:00. She has a ten-minute break at 10:00 and a half-hour break at 11:30. She has lunch during her long break. After class, Maria goes to work. She works at Maison Blanche, a busy department store downtown. She works in the hat department. She likes her work and she likes to talk to the customers. She works very hard. At 5:00, she finishes work. Then, she takes the bus back home. It takes her a half hour to get home.

In the evening, Maria usually has dinner with her cousin. When her cousin works late, Maria eats alone. She likes to listen to the radio while she eats. After dinner, she does the dishes. Then, she studies. She usually goes to bed late because she has a lot of homework.

All in all, Maria is a very busy person. She works hard and studies hard. She misses her family in Mexico, but she has a good life.

9

10

11

Composition 1

Instructions for Student's Composition

1. Write a composition about your daily activities on 8½ × 11 loose-leaf notebook paper. Give your composition a title.

2. Write five paragraphs. Put the following information in your paragraphs:

   Paragraph 1. Introduce yourself. Where do you live? What do you do?
   Paragraph 2. Tell about your morning activities (before work or school).
   Paragraph 3. Tell about the main part of your day.
   Paragraph 4. Tell about your evening activities.
   Paragraph 5. Conclude with several general points.

   Remember to leave margins and indent for each paragraph.

3. Take as many structures, ideas, and words from Model 1 as you can use in your composition.

4. Your composition should look like this:

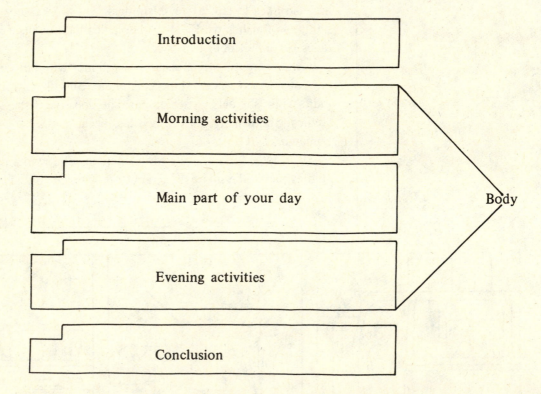

Unit 2

Composition Focus: Friendly Letter in Conversational Tone, Using Description and Narration

Organizational Focus: Spatial Order (1st paragraph) Shift of Conversational Focus (the setting, I, you)

Grammatical Focus: Present Continuous Tense Quantifiers, e.g., *most, all, several*

Reading 2

A LETTER TO A FRIEND

February 12, 1989

Dear Carmen,

It is early afternoon and I am sitting in a small restaurant close to my work. It is a nasty day in New Orleans. It is raining and I am feeling homesick. I am thinking of you and all of my friends in Mexico. I miss everyone. Outside, the sidewalks are crowded with people. All of them are wearing coats and carrying umbrellas. Everyone is in a hurry to get to a dry place. Buses and cars are moving up and down the street. Inside, it is warm and pleasant. There are two old women at the table next to mine. One of them is wearing a funny hat. They are gossiping and laughing. I like their New Orleans accent. A young man is sitting at a small table near the window. He is eating a piece of pecan pie. It looks delicious. You know, the food in New Orleans is wonderful.

I am fine. I am learning a lot in my classes. I like most of my teachers and classmates. One of my classmates is my new boyfriend! His name is Bruno and he is very nice. I attend classes every morning, I work every afternoon, and I study every evening. I don't have much free time, but I like my life in New Orleans.

I hope that you are well and happy. How is school? How is your English? Can you read my letter? Please write soon. I enjoy your letters with news from home. My cousin, Sylvia, sends her regards.

Your friend,

Maria

Sample Envelope

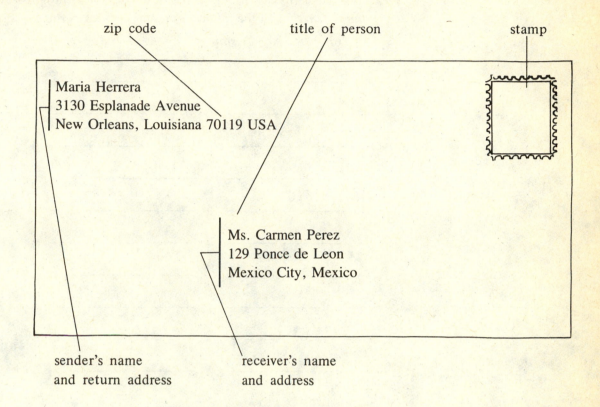

zip code   title of person   stamp

Maria Herrera
3130 Esplanade Avenue
New Orleans, Louisiana 70119 USA

Ms. Carmen Perez
129 Ponce de Leon
Mexico City, Mexico

sender's name
and return address

receiver's name
and address

Note to the student:
>   There are different ways to conclude or close a letter:
>
>   *Love* (when you write to a special friend or relative)
>   *Sincerely* (when you write a business letter or write to a friend)
>   *Your friend* (when you write to a friend)
>   *Your cousin* (when you write to a cousin)
>
>   Your teacher can explain other possibilities.

Exercise A: Present Continuous Tense

Please list all verbs in Reading 2 that show action in progress (the *present continuous tense*). List the infinitive and the present participle forms.

Example: sit   sitting

1. _____   _____

2. _____   _____

3. _____   _____

4. _____   _____

5. _____   _____

6. _____   _____

7. _____   _____

8. _____   _____

9. _____   _____

10. _____   _____

Exercise B: Quantifiers

Please complete the following sentences with *words of quantity*. Find each sentence in Reading 2 and complete it with the same words of quantity.

1. I am thinking of you and _____ my friends in Mexico.

2. The streets are crowded with people. _____ are wearing coats and carrying umbrellas.

3. _____ is in a hurry to get to a dry place.

4. There are _____ old women at the table next to mine.

5. _____ is wearing a funny hat.

6. I am learning _____ in my classes.

7. I like _____ my teachers and classmates.

8. _____ my classmates is my new boyfriend!

9. I attend classes _____ morning, I work _____

    afternoon, and I study _____ evening.

10. I don't have _____ free time, but I like my life in New Orleans.

Exercise C: Spatial Terms

Please reread ''A Letter to a Friend.'' Underline the words for space. These are the little words that tell you *where*. Then, complete the sentences below with the words in the list below. Make the meaning the same as in Reading 2.

up and down	*close to*	*at*
in	*near*	*outside*
next to	*inside*	

1. I am sitting _____ a small restaurant.

2. The restaurant is _____ my work.

3. _____, the sidewalks are crowded with people.

4. Buses and cars are moving _____ the street.

5. _____, it is warm and pleasant.

6. There are two old women at the table _____ mine.

7. A young man is sitting _____ a small table.

8. His table is _____ the window.

Exercise D: Spatial Order

Please reorganize the following groups of sentences. Put them into correct *order*. The order is according to *space*. The information is not from Reading 2.

1. There is a comfortable chair beside the table.

2. As you enter the room, you will see a large table.

3. In front of the chair, there is a small table.

4. On the small table, there is an ashtray.

   The correct order is _____, _____, _____, _____.

1. I am having lunch in the restaurant.

2. Next to my table, there are two pretty girls.

3. There is a restaurant near my school.

4. I am sitting near the window.

   The correct order is _____, _____, _____, _____.

1. In the back of the room, there are also windows.

2. Near the center of the room, there are many small desks.

3. I study in a pleasant classroom.

4. In the front of the room, there are large windows.

   The correct order is _____, _____, _____, _____.

1. Near the children, there is a small fountain.

2. There are trees and flowers around me.

3. Under the trees, children are playing.

4. I am sitting in a park.

   The correct order is _____, _____, _____, _____.

1. I am a waitress in a small restaurant.

2. It is warm and pleasant here.

3. People are walking in the snow.

4. Outside, it is snowing.

   The correct order is _____, _____, _____, _____.

Notes and Questions on the *Organization* of Reading 2

Part A: Paragraphs

Reading 2 is a friendly letter. "Friendly" letter means that it is not a business letter. The form of a business letter is different. (See Unit 6.) Reading 2 has three paragraphs. Go back to Reading 2. Be sure that you see three paragraphs. Notice the date, the name of the receiver of the letter, and the name of the writer of the letter. The following questions will help you understand the *system of paragraphs* in Reading 2:

1. The first paragraph describes something. What does it describe? Why do you think that Maria begins with a description? Will a description give Carmen a "picture" of Maria's daily life?

2. What information does the second paragraph give? Does it give more description? Who is the subject of the second paragraph?

3. What does the third paragraph do? Why is it last? Who is it about?

Is there really an *introduction*, a *body*, and a *conclusion* in a friendly letter? Is it the same as Reading 1 or Model 1? It isn't really, is it?

Part B: Order

Let's look at the first paragraph in Reading 2. The following questions will help you understand the *order* of the first paragraph. Remember that the word *order* refers to what is first, what is second, etc.

1. What is the place? Does Maria begin with the details or with general information?

2. Does Maria describe the outside or the inside first? Why?

3. Where does the description of the inside begin?

4. Does Maria describe the furniture inside? The color of the walls? How does she describe the inside?

5. Where is everyone?

If the description tells ''where,'' the writer is using **space order** or **spatial order**. Think of different descriptions that might need spatial order.

Notice these **words for space** in Reading 2:

in	*inside*
close to	*at*
outside	*next to*
up and down	*near*

Think of other words for space. Ask your teacher for help. Now, go on to Model 2.

1

2

3

4

LAKE
COLLEGE   NEIGHBORHOOD

5

6

Model 2

A LETTER TO A RELATIVE

July 9, 1989

Dear Dominick,

It is Saturday afternoon and I am sitting in Audubon Park. It is a hot summer day in New Orleans. I am sitting under a huge oak tree and I am thinking of you. The park is crowded with people. Many of them are strolling through the park. To my left, some children are playing. They are swinging on the swings. To my right, Roberto and some of our friends are playing soccer. They want me to play after I finish this letter. Several of the friends are classmates from Lake College. The others are friends from our neighborhood in New Orleans. They are good friends, but I prefer our friends from the old neighborhood in Rome. New friends are not the same, are they?

I am fine, but I miss you and my other old friends. You are a good cousin and a good friend! I am enjoying my

classes and I am learning a lot. Most of my classmates
are nice. One of my classmates is especially nice. She is
also very pretty. Her name is Maria and she is my new
girlfriend! I attend classes five mornings a week and I
work at a music store three afternoons a week. I like my
job.

How are you? I hope you are well and happy. How is
San Francisco? Roberto and I hope to visit you again
soon. When will you come to New Orleans for a visit? I
want you to meet Maria. Roberto says to tell you "Hello."
Please write soon. I always enjoy your letters.

Your cousin and friend,

Bruno

Composition 2

Instructions for Student's Composition

1. Write a letter to a friend or relative. Write on your own personal stationery, an aerogram, or a piece of 8½ × 11 loose-leaf notebook paper. Make it a real letter. Address the front of the aerogram or an envelope to put the letter in.

2. Follow the form for a friendly letter. Write the date in the top right corner of your paper. To the left, 1½ inches down, write *Dear* _____. Write three paragraphs. Put the following information in your paragraphs:

   Paragraph 1. Describe where you are. What are you doing? What are other people doing?
   Paragraph 2. Talk about your daily life.
   Paragraph 3. Talk about the person you are writing to.

   Then, conclude the letter with *Sincerely* or some other appropriate conclusion. Then, write your first name.

3. Take what you need from Model 2. Let it help you with grammar, vocabulary, and ideas.

4. Your letter should look like this:

_____(Date)_____

Dear _____ ,

Description of place

Talk about yourself

Talk about the person you are writing to

Sincerely,
(Your name)

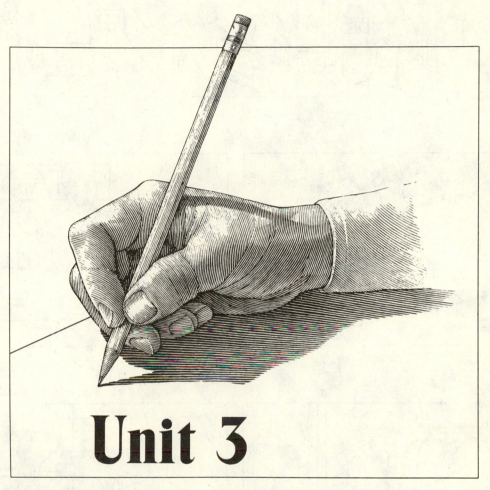

Unit 3

Composition Focus: Description

Organizational Focus: Classification

Grammatical Focus: Simple Present Tense
Future with *be going to*
Predicate Adjectives

Reading 3

MY FRIEND, ROBERTO

Roberto is one of my good friends. He is also my brother! We go to school together. We play soccer together. We live together. We even share a bedroom. We also share our parents! I think that we are going to be longtime friends. We are certainly going to be longtime brothers!

Roberto is 21 years old. He is about 5 feet, 9 inches tall. His face is long and narrow. His eyes are green. His hair is light brown. He doesn't look very Italian. He smiles a lot and usually has a friendly look on his face. He isn't fat and he isn't thin. His build is average. He plays soccer and baseball, so he stays in shape. He doesn't like to dress up. He likes to wear jeans and T-shirts.

Roberto has a pleasant personality. He is fairly outgoing, but he is also very sensitive. He worries about our parents because they work so hard. He also worries about our grandparents because they are old. My grandfather is also ill. He often writes to them. He is my older brother, but my English is better than his. He is a little

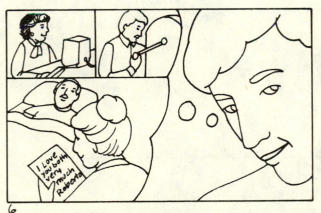

sensitive about that, too! Roberto is crazy about strawberry ice cream and baseball.

Roberto's future plans are not very definite. First, he is going to improve his English. Then, he is going to study physical education. He wants to be a high school coach. After that, I don't know what he is going to do. He has a girlfriend and he likes her very much. Is he going to marry her? I don't know, but I hope so. I want him to be happy. He is a good person and a true friend.

8

9

10

Exercise A: *Be*/Predicate Adjectives

Please rewrite the following sentences. Use *is* or *are*. Put the adjective after the verb and put the noun before the verb. Use *his* at the beginning of each sentence.

Example: He has a long face.
His face is long.

1. He has a narrow face.

    _____

2. He has green eyes.

    _____

3. He has light hair.

    _____

4. He has brown hair.

    _____

5. He has a friendly look.

    _____

6. He has a pleasant smile.

    _____

7. He has a pleasant personality.

    _____

8. He has an average build.

    _____

9. He has interesting ideas.

    _____

10. He has indefinite plans.

    _____

Exercise B: *Be going to*

Please complete the following. Write full sentences. Use *He is going to* at the beginning of each sentence. The time is *future*. You are writing about some-one's future plans, but not about Roberto's.

> *Example:* return to his country
> *He is going to return to his country.*

1. become an engineer

   _____

2. improve his English

   _____

3. buy a house

   _____

4. look for another job

   _____

5. get married

   _____

6. go to evening school

   _____

7. get a college degree

   _____

8. settle down

   _____

9. study more English

   _____

10. take a trip

    _____

Exercise C: Cohesion (Connection)

Please complete the following sentences. Take words from the list below. Use each one only one time. The words in the list *connect* the ideas of different parts of sentences or of different sentences.

after that	*also*	*then*
and	*so*	*that*
but	*first*	*because*

1. He is one of my friends and his is _____ my brother.

2. We go to school together _____ we play soccer together.

3. I think _____ we are going to be longtime friends.

4. Roberto plays soccer and baseball, _____ he stays in shape.

5. He is fairly outgoing, _____ he is very sensitive.

6. He worries about our parents _____ they work so hard.

7. Roberto has some future plans. _____, he is going to improve his English.

8. He is going to improve his English. _____, he is going to study physical education.

9. He is going to get a college degree. _____ I don't know what he is going to do.

Exercise D: Punctuation

Reading 3 is repeated below without **punctuation**. Please read through it and add **commas** and **periods**. The grammar and the capital letters will help you. Go back to Reading 3 and check your work after you finish.

MY FRIEND ROBERTO

Roberto is one of my good friends He is also my brother We go to school together We play soccer together We live together We even share a bedroom We also share our parents I think that we are going to be longtime friends We are certainly going to be longtime brothers

Roberto is 21 years old He is about 5 feet 9 inches tall His face is long and narrow His eyes are green His hair is light brown He doesn't look very Italian He smiles a lot and usually has a friendly look on his face He isn't fat and he isn't thin His build is average He plays soccer and baseball so he stays in shape He doesn't like to dress up He likes to wear jeans and T-shirts

Roberto has a pleasant personality He is fairly outgoing but he is also very sensitive He worries about our parents because they work so hard He also worries about our grandparents because they are old My grandfather is also ill He often writes to them He is my older brother but my English is better than his He is a little sensitive about that too Roberto is crazy about strawberry ice cream and baseball

Roberto's future plans are not very definite First he is going to improve his English Then he is going to study physical education He wants to be a high school coach After that I don't know what he is going to do He has a girlfriend and he likes her very much Is he going to marry her? I don't know but I hope so I want him to be happy He is a good person and a good friend

---

Notes and Questions on the *Organization* of Reading 3

Part A: Paragraphs

Reading 3 is a description of a person. There are four paragraphs. Read them again. Notice the differences in the content of the paragraphs. The following questions will help you understand the *system of paragraphs* in Reading 3:

1. Where do you begin to get details about Roberto? Why is the first paragraph there, then? What does it do?

2. What kind of details do you get in the second paragraph?

3. What information does the third paragraph give you? How is it different from the second paragraph?

4. Does the fourth paragraph give you some new information? How does it serve as a conclusion?

A *conclusion* can repeat, summarize, emphasize, or add to the information in a composition. Sometimes, it does a little of everything.

Part B: Order

The following questions and comments will help you understand the order of Reading 3:

1. What is the general topic of Reading 3? It is true that "Roberto" is the topic, but what is the more general topic?

2. That general topic is divided into two parts, or categories. What are they? (Look at the second and third paragraphs.)

3. Look at the second paragraph. Notice that the writer begins the physical description with the head and face (after giving age and height).

4. Is it possible to change the order of the two categories? Can personality come before physical appearance? Which order do you prefer?

A division of a general topic into subtopics, or parts, or classes is called *classification*. Think of topics that you might classify. (There are many examples in science.) Next, go on to Model 3.

1

APPLICATION
for
MAISON BLANCHE

AGE: 19
HEIGHT: 1.6 meters

EYES: BROWN
HAIR: BROWN
REMARKS:

2

3

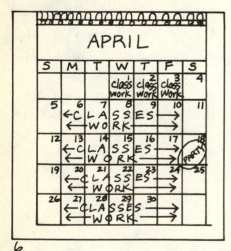

4

WAR
BREAKS
OUT!

STOCK
MARKET
CRASHES

FIRE DESTROYS
HOME

5

APRIL

S	M	T	W	T	F	S
			1 class work	2 class work	3 class work	4
5	6	7	8	9	10	11
	←CLASSES→ WORK					
12	13	14	15	16	17	18 PARTY
	←CLASSES→ WORK					
19	20	21	22	23	24	25
	←CLASSES→ WORK					
26	27	28	29	30		
	←CLASSES→ WORK					

6

PSYCHOLOGY
ENGLISH
POLITICAL
SCIENCE

7

EXIT

THANK-
YOU!,
MARIA!

8

Model 3

MY GIRLFRIEND, MARIA

Maria Herrera is a very nice person. She is a friend from school. She is also my girlfriend. I think that we are going to be friends for a long time.

Maria is 19 years old. She is about 5 feet, 3 inches tall. Her eyes are brown and her face is round. Her hair is brown and curly. She wears it short. She has a very pleasant smile and she always has a twinkle in her eye. She doesn't wear glasses. She thinks that she is fat, but she isn't. She is always on a diet. She always looks nice. She wears dresses and skirts to school because she goes to work in a department store after class. She can't wear jeans to work.

Maria has a wonderful personality. She is a serious person, but she also likes to have a good time. She likes people and she likes parties. She doesn't have much time for fun, but she is always ready for a party on Saturday night. Maria is very smart. She is a good student and she gets good grades. She knows a lot about politics and psychology. She likes to discuss these subjects, but she doesn't make other people feel inferior. She is patient and kind. All of these qualities make her a good salesperson in the hat department at Maison Blanche. Plus, she is crazy about hats!

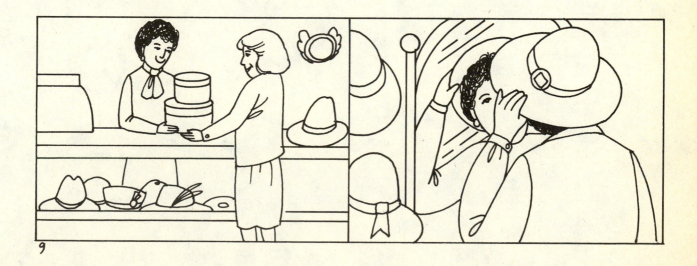

Maria's future plans are a little uncertain. However, she thinks that she is going to get a bachelor's degree in psychology. Then, perhaps she will go on to graduate school. I am sure that she will be successful. I also hope that she is going to include me in her future plans!

Composition 3

Instructions for Student's Composition

1. Write a composition about a friend on 8½ × 11 loose-leaf notebook paper. Describe your friend. Give your composition a title.

2. Write four paragraphs. Put the following information in your paragraphs:

   Paragraph 1. Introduce your friend. How do you know him/her? What do you think of the friendship?

   Paragraph 2. Describe your friend physically: age, color of hair, color of eyes, face, body, clothes, etc.

   Paragraph 3: Describe your friend's personality.

   Paragraph 4. Conclude with your friend's future plans. Give your feelings about you friend's future.

3. Take what you need from Model 3. Let it help you with grammar, vocabulary, and ideas.

4. Your composition should look like this:

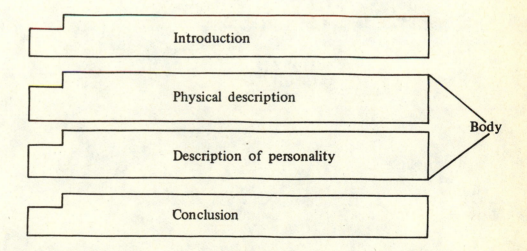

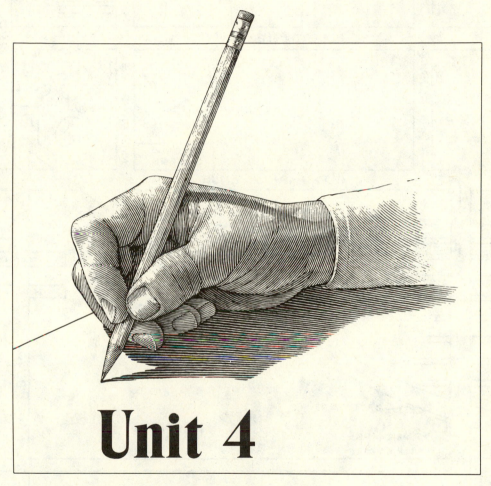

Unit 4

Composition Focus: Process Description

Organizational Focus: Chronological Order

Grammatical Focus: Imperatives
Modals: *can, should, will, might, may, must*

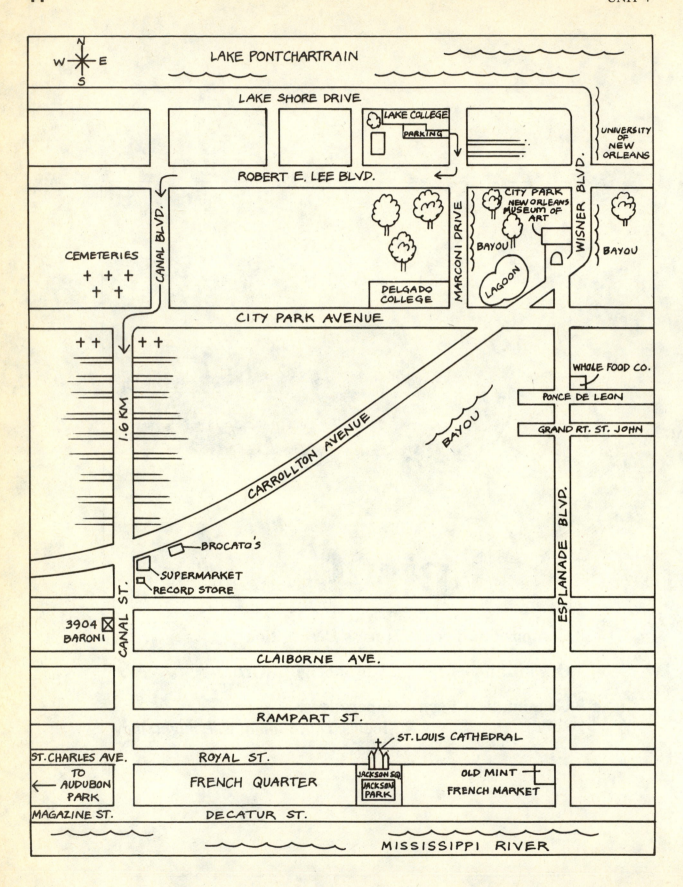

N
W · E
S

LAKE PONTCHARTRAIN

LAKE SHORE DRIVE

LAKE COLLEGE
PARKING

UNIVERSITY
OF
NEW
ORLEANS

ROBERT E. LEE BLVD.

CANAL BLVD.

CITY PARK
NEW ORLEANS
MUSEUM OF
ART

WISNER BLVD.

CEMETERIES
+ + +
+ +

BAYOU

BAYOU

MARCONI DRIVE

DELGADO
COLLEGE

LAGOON

CITY PARK AVENUE

WHOLE FOOD CO.

1.6 KM

+ +   + +

CARROLLTON AVENUE

BAYOU

PONCE DE LEON

GRAND RT. ST. JOHN

ESPLANADE BLVD.

BROCATO'S

SUPERMARKET
RECORD STORE

CANAL ST.

3904
BARONI ⊠

CLAIBORNE AVE.

RAMPART ST.

ST. LOUIS CATHEDRAL

ST. CHARLES AVE.
TO
← AUDUBON
PARK

ROYAL ST.

FRENCH QUARTER

JACKSON SQ.
JACKSON
PARK

OLD MINT
FRENCH MARKET

MAGAZINE ST.

DECATUR ST.

MISSISSIPPI RIVER

Reading 4

A PARTY

Some people like to give parties, but everyone likes to go to them. Giving a party can be fun. It can be easy and inexpensive, too, if all of the guests bring something to eat or drink. Bruno and Roberto are going to have a party next Saturday night. Here are the directions to their house. Follow these directions. They will lead you from Lake College to their house by car. You can find your way there from your house if you know the location of Lake College.

From the parking lot of the school, turn right on Marconi Drive. Stay on Marconi for three short blocks. At the first traffic light, turn right again. This is Robert E. Lee Boulevard. Stay on Robert E. Lee for about three blocks. At the corner of Robert E. Lee and Canal Boulevard, turn left. Canal is a long street and you will need to stay on it for about a mile. At the cemeteries, Canal Boulevard will become Canal Street. At that point, you must jog right and then jog left. Be careful here. This intersection is very dangerous. You should stay on Canal Street for ten or twelve more blocks. Stop when you get to 3904 Canal Street. This is the place. Ring the bell and someone will let you in.

Bruno and Roberto hope that you will come. Bring something to eat or drink. You may also bring a friend. You might miss a good time if you don't come.

Exercise A: Imperatives

Please list all of the *simple imperatives* (no subject, no auxiliary) in Reading 4.

Example: Follow these directions.

1. _____

2. _____

3. _____

4. _____

5. _____

6. _____

7. _____

8. _____

9. _____

Exercise B: Modals

Rewrite each of the following sentences. Use the *modal auxiliary* in parentheses. After you finish, check your sentences with the same sentences in Reading 4.

1. Giving a party is fun.   (can)

   _____

2. It is easy and inexpensive, too.   (can)

   _____

3. The directions lead you from Lake College to their house.   (will)

   _____

4. You find your way there from your house.   (can)

   _____

5. You need to stay on Canal Boulevard for about a mile.   (will)

   _____

6. At the cemeteries, Canal Boulevard becomes Canal Street.   (will)

   _____

7. There, you jog right and left.   (must)

   _____

8. You stay on Canal Street for ten or twelve more blocks.   (should)

   _____

9. Someone lets you in.   (will)

   _____

10. You bring a friend.   (may)

   _____

Exercise C: Cohesion (Reference)

The italicized part of each sentence below refers the reader to another point of information. All of the sentences come from Reading 4. What is the *reference*? Please circle the letter below the sentence to show the correct reference.

1. Some people like to give parties, but everyone likes to go to *them*.
   What does *them* refer to?

   a. some people

   b. everyone

   c. parties

2. Giving a party can be fun. *It* can be easy and inexpensive, too, if all of the guests bring something to eat or drink.
   What does *it* refer to?

   a. giving a party

   b. something to eat

   c. something to drink

3. Bruno and Roberto are going to have a party next Saturday night. Here are the directions to *their* house. Follow these directions. *They* will lead you from Lake College to *their* house by car.

   What does *their* refer to?

   a. Bruno's house

   b. Roberto's house

   c. Bruno and Roberto's house

   What does *they* refer to?

   a. the directions to Bruno and Roberto's

   b. Bruno and Roberto

   c. the students at Lake College

4. Canal is a long street and you will need to stay on *it* for about a mile.
   What does *it* refer to?

   a. a long street

   b. Canal Boulevard

   c. a mile

5. At the cemeteries, Canal Boulevard will become Canal Street. *At that point*, you must jog right and then jog left.
   What does *at that point* refer to?

   a. where people are buried

   b. where Canal Boulevard becomes Canal Street

   c. where people jog

Exercise D: Chronological and Logical Order

Please reorganize the following groups of sentences. Put them into correct *order*. This order is according to *time* and *logic*.

1. First, leave the parking lot at Lake College.

2. At that traffic light, turn right.

3. You will now be on Robert E. Lee Boulevard.

4. It is three blocks from the parking lot to the first traffic light.

   The correct order is _____, _____, _____, _____.

1. At the cemeteries, jog right and then left.

2. At the corner of Robert E. Lee and Canal Boulevard, turn left on Canal.

3. Drive along Canal until you get to the cemeteries.

4. Stay on Robert E. Lee for about three blocks.

   The correct order is _____, _____, _____, _____.

1. Drive along Canal Street for another ten or twelve blocks.

2. This is the place!

3. At the cemeteries, Canal Boulevard will become Canal Street.

4. Stop when you get to 3904 Canal Street.

   The correct order is _____, _____, _____, _____.

1. Please come and bring a friend.

2. You have the directions to Bruno and Roberto's house.

3. If you follow these directions, you can find your way there.

4. You might also bring something to eat or drink.

   The correct order is _____, _____, _____, _____.

Notes and Questions on the *Organization* of Reading 4

Part A: Paragraphs

Reading 4 describes how to do something. "How to" is a process. Therefore, Reading 4 is called a process description. There are three paragraphs. The following questions will help you understand the *system of paragraphs* in Reading 4:

1. Where does the process begin?

2. What does the first paragraph do, then? Where does the reader get the topic of the composition? How does the writer lead to the topic?

3. Where do the directions end? In other words, where does the process stop?

4. What does the last paragraph do?

   The first paragraph usually introduces the topic, or subject, of the composition. Therefore, it is called the **introduction**. It leads the reader to the main part of the composition.

Part B: Order

Let's look at the second paragraph in Reading 4. The following questions and comments will help you understand the order:

1. Should the partygoer leave the parking lot before or after driving down Marconi Drive?

2. Which is first—driving west on Robert E. Lee or south on Canal Boulevard?

3. Does the partygoer drive down Canal Boulevard before or after jogging right and left onto Canal Street?

4. The order is *time*, isn't it? Is the time order first to last or last to first? Notice the time words in the second paragraph.

5. If the process is described in the second paragraph, is *time* necessary in the first and third paragraphs? Why not?

   Process descriptions usually need time order. Think of other kinds of topics that might use time order. After you do this, please go on to Model 4.

Model 4

BRUNO'S CHEESE PIE

Bruno Baroni likes to cook. He is a good cook. Everyone in his family says so. He likes to cook Italian food, but his favorite recipe is one from Maria, his Mexican girlfriend. This recipe is for cheese pie. He is preparing it for the party tonight. Here is the recipe.

First, butter the bottom of a round baking dish. Then, put flour tortillas around the bottom. Let them come up the sides of the dish, too. Next, chop one large tomato, one small can of chili peppers, and one onion. Put the chopped tomato, peppers, and onion on the tortillas. After that, beat together 3 eggs, 3 tablespoons of flour, 1 teaspoon of salt, ½ teaspoon of baking powder, and ½ cup of milk. Then, you should fold in 1 cup of grated cheese. Next, pour the mixture into the dish over the chopped tomato, peppers, and onion. Finally, put the dish in the oven. Don't cover the dish. Bake the cheese pie for 45 minutes at 350 degrees. The pie will serve 4 people.

7

8

9

After you take the pie out of the oven, you will need to let it cool for about 30 minutes. Arrange slices of avocado in a circle on top of the pie. Add a few spoonfuls of taco sauce. Cut it in wedges and serve it to your guests. They will enjoy it. Bruno and Roberto's guests will, too!

10

11

Composition 4

Instructions for Student's Composition

1. Write a composition on 8½ × 11 loose-leaf notebook paper. Tell someone how to do or make something. You might write out a recipe or tell someone how to build something. Give your composition a title.

2. Write three paragraphs. Put the following information in your paragraphs:

    Paragraph 1. Introduce your idea. What are you talking about? Can people use it?

    Paragraph 2. Describe the process. What comes first? What is second? What is next? etc.

    Paragraph 3. What is the end of the process? Conclude with some general points.

    Be sure to leave margins and indent for each paragraph.

3. Take what you need from Model 4. Let it help you with grammar, vocabulary, and ideas.

4. Your composition should look like this:

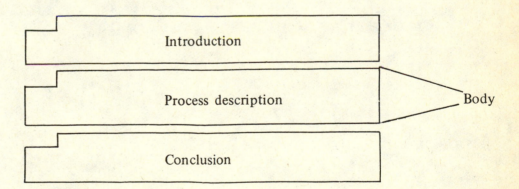

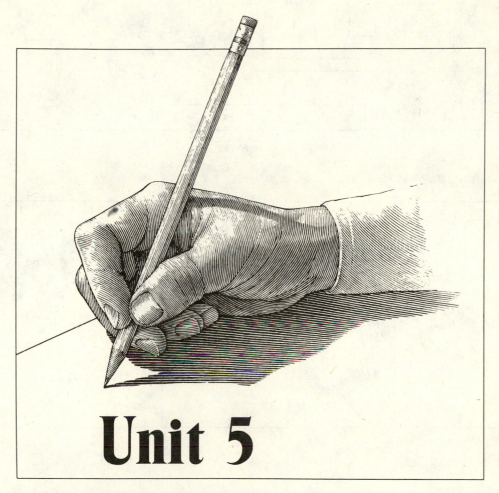

Unit 5

Composition Focus: Narration

Organizational Focus: Chronological Order

Grammatical Focus: Simple Past Tense
Objects: Direct and Indirect

YESTERDAY

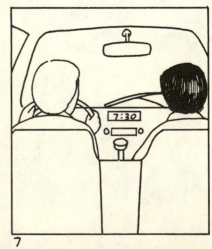

Reading 5

YESTERDAY

Yesterday was a typical day for Bruno. It was long and tiring, but it was interesting. In the morning, he went to class. In the afternoon, he went to work. In the evening, he had dinner with his family and studied. That is the way his life goes.

Bruno's alarm rang at 6:00. He jumped out of bed and did some exercises. By that time, it was his turn in the bathroom. He took a shower, shaved, and brushed his teeth. He thought about his girlfriend, Maria, while he brushed his teeth. After he got dressed, he went to the kitchen for breakfast. His mother had it ready for him. He ate his usual breakfast—toast and fruit with coffee. After breakfast, he cleaned up the kitchen and did the dishes while his mother got ready for work. At 7:30, he and his brother, Roberto, were ready to leave for school.

Traffic was light, so Bruno and Roberto drove to school in fifteen minutes. Roberto went straight to class and Bruno went to the library. He asked the librarian some questions and looked up some information for his chemistry class. Then, he rushed to the cafeteria to meet Maria. They had a quick cup of coffee before their nine o'clock classes. After his eleven o'clock class, he met Roberto and Roberto's girlfriend, Sylvia, for lunch. He couldn't have lunch with Maria because she doesn't finish her classes until 1:00. By that time, he has to go to work.

8

9

10

The rest of the day passed as usual. After lunch, Roberto dropped Bruno off at the music store where he works. He works there three afternoons a week. Bruno sold a clarinet, two guitars, and a violin before the afternoon was over. He got off work at 5:30 and took the bus home. Nobody was home when he arrived, so he started dinner. Spaghetti was ready and on the table when his parents and Roberto got home. They were hungry and ready to eat! After dinner, Bruno relaxed for a few minutes and then started his homework. He studied until midnight and fell into bed. He was asleep before his head hit the pillow. It was a typical day!

11

12

13

14

15

Exercise A: Simple Past Tense

Part 1

Please reread Reading 5. Look for verbs in the *simple past tense*. List them below. List the verb and its past tense form. (There are 27 different verbs in the simple past tense; list each verb only one time.)

Example: *make   made*

1. _____
2. _____
3. _____
4. _____
5. _____
6. _____
7. _____
8. _____
9. _____
10. _____
11. _____
12. _____
13. _____
14. _____

15. _____
16. _____
17. _____
18. _____
19. _____
20. _____
21. _____
22. _____
23. _____
24. _____
25. _____
26. _____
27. _____

Part 2

Please change these sentences to the *past*. Change the verb to the simple past tense. If there is a present time word, change it to a past time word.

> *Example:*   Every morning, Bruno goes to class.
> *Yesterday morning, Bruno went to class.*

1. Every day, Bruno gets up at 6:00.

   _____

2. Every morning, his alarm rings at 6:00.

   _____

3. He jumps out of bed and does exercises every morning.

   _____

4. He takes a shower, shaves, and brushes his teeth.

   _____

5. He thinks about Maria while he brushes his teeth.

   _____

6. After he gets dressed, he goes to the kitchen for breakfast.

   _____

7. After breakfast, he cleans up the kitchen and does the dishes.

   _____

8. Traffic is light, so Bruno and Roberto drive to school in fifteen minutes.

   _____

9. Bruno asks the librarian some questions and looks up some information.

   _____

10. Then, he rushes to the cafeteria to meet Maria for a quick cup of coffee.

    _____

11. At noon every day, Bruno meets Sylvia and Roberto for lunch.

    _____

12. Some afternoons, he works from 1:00 to 5:30.

_____

13. Every evening, Bruno has dinner with his family.

_____

14. Some evenings, he cooks dinner for everyone.

_____

15. Some nights, he studies until midnight.

_____

Exercise B: Objects

Please answer the following questions with information from Reading 5. Pay attention to the position of the *objects*.

1. What did Bruno do after he jumped out of bed?

   _____

2. Who did he think about while he brushed his teeth?

   _____

3. Why did he go to the kitchen?

   _____

4. How long did it take Bruno and Roberto to get to school?

   _____

5. What did Bruno do in the library?

   _____

6. Why did Bruno rush to the cafeteria?

   _____

7. Who did Bruno meet for lunch?

   _____

8. Why didn't he have lunch with Maria?

   _____

9. How did Bruno get to work?

   _____

10. What did Bruno do before the afternoon was over?

   _____

Exercise C: Chronological Order

Please reorganize the following sentences. Put them into correct *time order*. (Another name for time order is *chronological order*. It is the same.)

1. In the afternoon, he went to work.

2. That is the way his life goes.

3. In the evening, he relaxed a little.

4. In the morning, Bruno went to class.

The correct order is _____, _____, _____, _____.

1. After he jumped out of bed, he did some exercises.

2. After his shower, he got dressed.

3. Bruno's alarm clock rang at 6:00.

4. Next, he took a shower.

The correct order is _____, _____, _____, _____.

1. Bruno left for school at 7:30.

2. By 9:00, he was in class.

3. Before class, he went to the library.

4. It took him only about 15 minutes to get there.

The correct order is _____, _____, _____, _____.

1. After lunch, Roberto drove him to work.

2. At noon, Bruno met Sylvia and Roberto for lunch.

3. They usually eat in the cafeteria.

4. He works in a music store three afternoons a week.

The correct order is _____, _____, _____, _____.

1. He immediately started cooking dinner.

2. He took the bus home.

3. Bruno got off work at 5:30.

4. When he got home, nobody was there.

The correct order is _____, _____, _____, _____.

Exercise D: Capitalization

Reading 5 is repeated below without *capital letters*. Please read through it and add capital letters. The grammar and the punctuation will help you. Go back to Reading 5 and check your work after you finish.

yesterday

yesterday was a typical day for bruno. it was long and tiring, but it was interesting. in the morning, he went to class. in the afternoon, he went to work. in the evening, he had dinner with his family and studied. that is the way his life goes.

bruno's alarm rang at 6:00. he jumped out of bed and did some exercises. by that time, it was his turn in the bathroom. he took a shower, shaved, and brushed his teeth. he thought about his girlfriend, maria, while he brushed his teeth. after he got dressed, he went to the kitchen for breakfast. his mother had it ready for him. he ate his usual breakfast—toast and fruit with coffee. after breakfast, he cleaned up the kitchen and did the dishes while his mother got ready for work. at 7:30, he and his brother, roberto, were ready to leave for school.

traffic was light, so bruno and roberto drove to school in fifteen minutes. roberto went straight to class and bruno went to the library. he asked the librarian some questions and looked up some information for his chemistry class. then, he rushed to the cafeteria to meet maria. they had a quick cup of coffee before their nine o'clock classes. after his eleven o'clock class, he met roberto and roberto's girlfriend, sylvia, for lunch. bruno couldn't have lunch with maria because she doesn't finish her classes until 1:00. by that time, he has to go to work.

the rest of the day passed as usual. after lunch roberto dropped bruno off at the music store where he works. he works there three afternoons a week. bruno sold a clarinet, two guitars, and a violin before the afternoon was over. he got off at 5:30 and took the bus home. nobody was home when he arrived, so he started dinner. spaghetti was ready and on the table when his parents and roberto got home. they were hungry and ready to eat! after dinner, bruno relaxed for a few minutes and then started his homework. he studied until midnight and fell into bed. he was asleep before his head hit the pillow. it was a typical day.

Notes and Questions on the *Organization* of Reading 5

Part A: Paragraphs

Reading 5 tells a kind of story. It is the story of someone's daily life. The writer explains his daily life by explaining a typical day in the past. There are four paragraphs. You might expect five paragraphs: an introduction, "morning," "afternoon," "evening," and a conclusion. Look carefully to understand the organization of Reading 5. Look to see how it is divided into paragraphs. The following questions will help you understand the *system of paragraphs* in Reading 5:

1. In the first paragraph, how does the writer divide the day?

2. Is the second paragraph about the morning?

3. What is the third paragraph about?

4. Where do you get information on the afternoon? On the evening?

5. How, then, is the day really divided?

6. How is the conclusion different from the other readings? The conclusion of the day is the conclusion of the composition, isn't it?

Sometimes, the **conclusion** of a composition is the end of the main part, or **body**. In Reading 5, the last part of the body is also the conclusion.

Part B: Order

By now, you probably already understand the order of Reading 5. The following questions will help you be sure:

1. How much time does the second paragraph cover?

2. How much time does the third paragraph cover? Is the time before or after the time in the second paragraph?

3. How much time does the last paragraph cover? Is the time before or after the time in the third paragraph?

4. *Look* for time words. Is the order from early to late or from late to early?

Remember that this kind of order is called **time order**, or **chronological order**. It is almost automatic to use time order in a composition on daily activities. Now, go on to Model 5.

Model 5

MRS. BARONI'S DAY

Friday was not a typical day for Mrs. Baroni, Roberto and Bruno's mother. It was difficult and frustrating. In the morning, she was late for work. In the afternoon, her boss got angry with her. By evening, she was exhausted. She is glad that most days are different.

Mrs. Baroni got up at 6:00 as usual. She took her turn in the bathroom first. Then she went straight to the kitchen. There, she fixed breakfast for her husband and her sons. After breakfast, her husband left for work, Bruno cleaned up the kitchen, and she got dressed. At 7:30, she said good-bye to Bruno and Roberto as they left for school. Then, she left the house and walked to the bus stop. So far, so good! She waited and waited at the bus stop. The bus finally came—about twenty minutes late. Then, on its way downtown, the bus broke down. All of the passengers had to get off and wait for another bus to come. She felt so nervous! Finally, she arrived at her office—thirty minutes late. Her boss wasn't very happy!

6

7

8

In the afternoon, her boss really got angry at her. Because she was upset in the morning, she forgot to mail an important form to the Internal Revenue Service. Friday was the deadline for the form. When her boss found out late in the afternoon, he said some very nasty things. Mrs. Baroni felt terrible. Later, he apologized. He knows that she really is a wonderful secretary and a valuable employee.

By the time Mrs. Baroni got home, she was exhausted. She told her family the whole story and they were very understanding. Bruno and Roberto offered to fix dinner while she took a long, hot bath. After her bath and a nice dinner, she felt much better. She went to bed early. She really deserved a good night's sleep!

9

10

11

12

13

Composition 5

Instructions for Student's Composition

1. Write a composition about yesterday or another past day on 8½ × 11 loose-leaf notebook paper. Describe your day.

2. Write four paragraphs. Don't forget to leave margins and indent for each paragraph. Put the following information in your paragraphs:

   Paragraph 1. What kind of day was this day? What was your main morning activity? What was your main afternoon activity? What was your main evening activity? How did you feel by evening?

   Paragraph 2. Describe your morning (early).

   Paragraph 3. Describe the next part of your day.

   Paragraph 4. Describe the rest of your day. Conclude with bedtime.

3. Use as much of Model 5 as you need. Let it help you with grammar, vocabulary, and ideas.

4. Your composition should look like this:

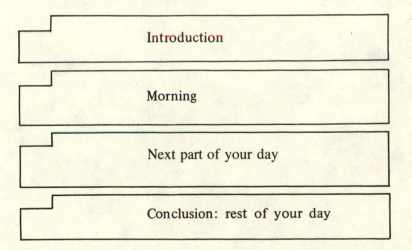

Introduction

Morning

Next part of your day

Conclusion: rest of your day

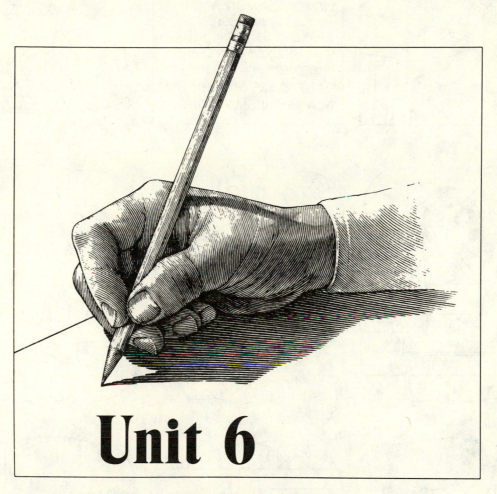

Unit 6

Composition Focus: Business Letter

Organizational Focus: Ranking of Requests

Grammatical Focus: Imperatives
Polite Requests with *would*

Reading 6

A BUSINESS LETTER

3904 Canal Street
New Orleans, Louisiana 70119
March 19, 1989

Greater New Orleans Tourist Commission
529 St. Ann Street
New Orleans, LA 70116

Dear Madam/Sir:

   I would like to request an interview for the position of secretary. I saw your advertisement in Friday's *Times Picayune*. I can type 80 words per minute. I can take shorthand at 120 words per minute. I am also able to use a computer. I have a diploma from a secretarial school in Rome, Italy. I once worked for five years as a secretary at the Italian Tourist Commission in Rome. I arrived in the New Orleans area four years ago. Now, I am working as a secretary for a large corporation downtown. I am interested in changing jobs. My English is good and my secretarial skills are excellent. I am also a responsible employee.

I would like to work for the Greater New Orleans Tourist Commission. I enjoyed my work with the tourist commission in Rome and I would like to return to that kind of office. I would be happy to give you a list of references and a complete resumé of my work experience.

Please contact me at the above address. Thank you very much.

Sincerely,

Sophia Baroni

Sophia Baroni

Exercise A: Comprehension

Please reread Reading 6. Next, answer the following questions. Then, check your *comprehension* of Reading 6. Go back to Reading 6 if you have trouble.

1. Where does Sophia Baroni live?
    a. 529 St. Ann Street
    b. Rome, Italy
    c. 3904 Canal Street
    d. Times Picayune

2. When did Sophia Baroni write the letter?
    a. four years ago
    b. five years ago
    c. Friday
    d. March 19, 1989

3. What is the zip code of the Greater New Orleans Tourist Commission?
    a. 70116
    b. 529
    c. 70119
    d. 3904

4. Why did Sophia Baroni write to the Greater New Orleans Tourist Commission?
    a. She wanted to improve her typing skills.
    b. She wanted to interview for a job.
    c. She once worked for the Italian Tourist Commission.
    d. She enjoyed her work in Rome.

5. What are Mrs. Baroni's secretarial skills?
    a. She can speak English.
    b. She can type, take shorthand, and use a computer.
    c. She is a responsible employee.
    d. She has a diploma from a secretarial school.

6. What is Mrs. Baroni's work experience?

a. She has a diploma from a secretarial school in Rome.

b. Her English is good, her secretarial skills are excellent, and she is a responsible employee.

c. She was a secretary in Rome for five years and she is with a large corporation in New Orleans now.

d. She arrived in New Orleans four years ago and found a job soon after that.

Exercise B: Indirect Requests with *would* + *like to*

Please rewrite the following sentences. Change *want to* to *would like to*. *Would like to* is more polite; it means *allow me* or *permit me* when you direct it to someone. It is an **indirect request**.

> *Example:*   I want to request an interview.
> *I would like to request an interview.*

1. I want to apply for a job.

    _____

2. I want to receive an application.

    _____

3. I want to get a diploma from a secretarial institute.

    _____

4. I want to work in the admissions office.

    _____

5. I want to study English at Lake College.

    _____

6. I want to work for Shell Oil Company.

    _____

7. I want to be a typist in your office.

    _____

8. I want to show you my references.

    _____

9. I want to send you a resumé of my work experience.

    _____

10. I want to thank you.

    _____

Exercise C: Direct Requests

Part 1

Please write one request for each of the following situations. Use the **imperative** with *please*. Use *me*, *to me*, or *for me* in each request. Use the verb in parentheses.

> *Example:* You have a question. You need an answer.   (answer)
> *Please answer a question for me.*

1. You need an application form.   (send)

   _____

2. You need some information.   (give)

   _____

3. You want to know the rules.   (explain)

   _____

4. You need a college catalog.   (send)

   _____

5. You want to receive a phone call or letter.   (contact)

   _____

6. You want to receive a letter at your home address.   (write)

   _____

7. You want to know the schedule.   (tell)

   _____

8. You know the answer. You want someone to ask a question.   (ask)

   _____

9. You want to understand the problem.   (explain)

   _____

10. You want to hear the news.   (tell)

    _____

Part 2

Please rewrite each request from Part 1 above. Use *Would you please* to make a polite direct request. Use your own paper.

> *Example:*   You have a question. You need an answer.   (answer)
> *Would you please answer a question for me.*

Exercise D: Ranking

Please reorder the information below. Rank it from most to least or least to most. Let your teacher help you decide on the "logic."

1. Population of U.S. Cities

Chicago, Illinois	2,997,155	_____
Los Angeles, California	3,022,247	_____
New York, New York	7,086,096	_____
Houston, Texas	1,725,617	_____

2. U.S. Postal Service Insurance

Insurance	Fee	
$25.01 to $50	$1.10	_____
$100.01 to $150	$1.80	_____
$0.01 to $25	$0.50	_____
$50.01 to $100	$1.40	_____

3. Principal Islands of the World

	Area (square miles)	
Madagascar	227,800	_____
Borneo	286,967	_____
New Guinea	316,856	_____
Greenland	840,000	_____

4. Telephone Numbers in New Orleans

Weather	(504) 525-8831	_____
Emergency (Police/Fire/Medical)	911	_____
Time	(504) 529-6111	_____
Travelers' Aid	(504) 525-8726	_____

Notes and Questions on the *Organization* of Reading 6

Part A: Paragraphs

Reading 6 is a business letter. Notice that the form is a little different from the friendly letter in Unit 2. Look at the differences. There are three paragraphs in Reading 6, in addition to the other parts (addresses, names, etc.). The following questions will help you understand Reading 6. The *system of paragraphs* in a business letter is different from a regular composition.

1. Does the first paragraph lead the reader to the main part in the second paragraph? If not, what does it do?

2. Is the second paragraph the main part, or body? If not, what is it? What does the reader get in the second paragraph?

3. What does the last paragraph do? What is last in the last paragraph?

   A letter is different from a composition. A letter has a kind of *conclusion*, but the *introduction* and *body* are not the same. There is no separate introduction. The writer begins the letter with the main point.

Part B: Order

The following questions will help you understand the *order of information* in Reading 6:

1. What does the writer request in the first paragraph? Why is the other information there?

2. What is the second paragraph about? How does that information connect to the first paragraph? What is the point of the second paragraph?

3. What does the writer request in the third paragraph?

4. Of the three paragraphs, which contains the most central point? How important are the other points, or requests?

   Think of other kinds of writing where you might *rank* information. Ranking means to put something first, then second, then third, etc. Writers often rank statistical information, such as the population of cities. How is ranking different from time order? Ask your teacher to explain. What might be a reason for ranking? With cities, for example, which one probably goes first? How do you decide? Now, go on to Model 6.

Model 6

A BUSINESS LETTER

3904 Canal Street
New Orleans, Louisiana 70119
July 25, 1989

Admissions Office
University of New Orleans
Lakefront
New Orleans, Louisiana 70148

Dear Madam/Sir:

Please send me an application for admission to the University of New Orleans. I have a diploma from Warren Easton High School in New Orleans. Now, I am taking general undergraduate courses at Lake College. This year, I completed my freshman courses in English composition, algebra, and chemistry. Next year, I will complete more general degree courses. I would like to begin my studies at the University of New Orleans in September 1990. My major field of interest is music.

I would also like to receive information on tuition and financial aid for students. Are there any special scholarships for music majors? In addition, I would like

to know more about the course requirements for a degree
in music. I hope that my courses at Lake College will
transfer to UNO.

  Please send all of this information as soon as possible.
It will help me plan my courses at Lake College for the
1989—90 school year. Please send it to the above address.
Thank you very much.

                        Sincerely,

                        Bruno Baroni

                        Bruno Baroni

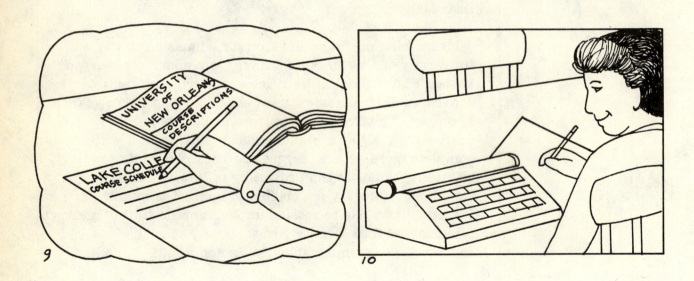

Composition 6

Instructions for Student's Composition

1. Write a business letter to a company or an institution. Write on 8½ × 11 plain white paper or loose-leaf notebook paper. Make it a real letter. Address an envelope for the letter.

2. Follow the form for a business letter. Write your address and the date in the top right corner. To the left, 1 inch down, write the name and address of the person who will receive the letter. Under that, ¼ inch down, write *Dear Madam*, *Dear Sir*, or *Dear* _____(full name)_____.

3. Write three paragraphs. Put the following information in your paragraphs:

   Paragraph 1. What do you want? Tell about yourself (if appropriate).
   Paragraph 2. Add any other requests or information.
   Paragraph 3. When do you want an answer? Where do you want to receive an answer? Say thank you.
   Then, conclude with *Sincerely* or *Sincerely yours*. Sign your full name.

4. Take what you need from Model 6. Let it help you with the form of your letter, grammar, vocabulary, and ideas.

5. Your letter should look like this:

```
                                                        ┌──────────────┐
                                                        │ Your address │
                                                        │ Date         │
                                                        └──────────────┘

                              ↕ 1 inch

┌──────────────────────────┐
│ Name/address of receiver │
└──────────────────────────┘

Dear _____ :
   ┌────────────────────────────────────────────────────┐
   │              Reason for writing                     │
   ├────────────────────────────────────────────────────┤
   │         Additional requests/information             │
   ├────────────────────────────────────────────────────┤
   │                 Conclusion                          │
   └────────────────────────────────────────────────────┘

                              Sincerely yours,
                              (Your name)
```

Unit 7

Composition Focus: Narration

Organizational Focus: Chronological Order

Grammatical Focus: Simple Past Tense
Predicate Infinitives (*to* + verb)

1

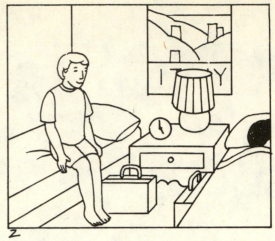

2

3

4

5

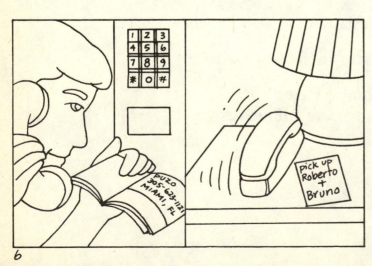

6

7

Reading 7

A TERRIBLE TRIP

My brother, Roberto, and I took a trip to Miami last summer. I will never forget it. We have some cousins in Miami and they wanted us to visit them. We thought about the beautiful beaches, so we decided to go. We also wanted to see our cousins, Angelo and Gina.

We had reservations on an early flight to Miami, so we got up before the sun rose. Roberto and I were all excited about the trip. Our father got up early to drive us to the airport. Our problems started on the way to the airport. We had a flat tire! This made us miss our flight and it made my father late for work. Roberto and I waited around the airport for another flight. We tried to call our cousins, but they weren't at home. They were on their way to the Miami Airport to pick us up! We finally boarded a flight and arrived in Miami four hours late. Of course, our cousins were not at the airport to meet us. We called their house and asked them to come back to the airport. They were very understanding. We waited outside for them. After a half hour, they drove up. When we saw them, we were so relieved! We apologized and apologized for all the trouble.

We stayed for a week and had a terrible time. It wasn't our cousins' fault, but nothing went right. It rained every day and we didn't go to the beach even one time. On the second day, Gina fell and hurt her leg. For the rest of the week, she couldn't walk. Then, Angelo had a car accident. He wasn't hurt, but their car was in the shop for the rest of the week.

When it was time to leave, we were both sad and happy. We wanted to return home, but we hated to leave Angelo and Gina. We said good-bye and begged them to visit us in New Orleans. We wanted to try again for a smooth visit. We had to take a taxi to the airport because their car was still in the shop. You will never guess what happened next! Yes, the taxi broke down on the way to the airport. Someone stopped to help and drove us to the airport. We arrived just in time to catch our plane. When we landed in New Orleans, our parents were at the airport to meet us. They couldn't believe our story!

10

11

12

Exercise A: Simple Past Tense

Please reread Reading 7. Look for verbs in the *simple past tense*. List them below. List the verb and its past tense form. (There are 31 different verbs; list each verb only once.)

1. take   took
2. _____
3. _____
4. _____
5. _____
6. _____
7. _____
8. _____
9. _____
10. _____
11. _____
12. _____
13. _____
14. _____
15. _____
16. _____

17. _____
18. _____
19. _____
20. _____
21. _____
22. _____
23. _____
24. _____
25. _____
26. _____
27. _____
28. _____
29. _____
30. _____
31. _____

Exercise B: Simple Past Tense

Please change these sentences to the *past*. Change the verb to the *simple past tense*. Change the present time words to past time words.

> *Example*:   My brother and I take a trip to Miami every year.
> *My brother and I took a trip to Miami last year.*

1. My cousins live in Miami all the time.

   _____

2. They want us to come to visit them every summer.

   _____

3. We talk about the beautiful beaches.

   _____

4. We get up before the sun rises every morning.

   _____

5. We are excited about our trip.

   _____

6. We have a flat tire once in a while.

   _____

7. My cousins honk the horn as they drive up.

   _____

8. It rains all the time.

   _____

9. We hug and kiss them.

   _____

10. Every summer, we stay for one week.

    _____

Exercise C: Predicate Infinitives

Combine each group below. Write only one sentence for each group. Every verb after the first one in each sentence should be in the *infinitive form* with *to*.

Example: They wanted us.
We came.
We visited them.
They wanted us to come to visit them.

1. We decided. We went.

_____

2. We wanted. We saw our cousins, Angelo and Gina.

_____

3. Our father got up. He drove us to the airport.

_____

4. Our cousins were not at the airport. Our cousins didn't meet us.

_____

5. We called their house. We asked them. They came back to the airport.

_____

6. We ran. We greeted them.

_____

7. After a week, it was time. We left.

_____

8. We hated. We left our cousins.

_____

9. We got into a taxi. We went to the airport.

_____

10. Someone stopped. Someone helped.

   _____

11. We arrived just in time. We caught our plane.

   _____

Exercise D: Cohesion (Connection)

Please reread Reading 5. Look for *words that connect* a subject and verb to another subject and verb. (Sometimes the second subject is not repeated.) Underline the connecting words: *and, so, because, when, but*. Next, combine each of the following groups of sentences. Use the connecting words in parentheses. Be careful with word order, punctuation, and capital letters.

Please combine these groups. Write a total of twelve sentences.

1. We have some cousins in Miami.   (and)
   They wanted us to visit them.

   _____

2. We thought about the beautiful beaches.   (so)
   We decided to go.

   _____

3. We had reservations on an early flight.   (so)
   We got up.   (before)
   The sun rose.

   _____

4. We tried to call our cousins.   (but)
   They weren't at home.

   _____

5. We finally boarded a flight.   (and)
   We arrived in Miami four hours late.

   _____

6. We saw them.   (when)
   We were so relieved!

   _____

7. It wasn't our cousins' fault.   (but)
   Nothing went right.

   _____

8. Angelo wasn't hurt in the accident.   (but)
    Their car was in the shop for the rest of the week.

    _____

9. It was time to leave.   (when)
    We were both sad and happy.

    _____

10. We had to take a taxi to the airport.   (because)
    Their car was still in the shop.

    _____

11. Someone stopped to help.   (and)
    Someone drove us to the airport.

    _____

12. We landed in New Orleans.   (when)
    Our parents were at the airport to meet us.

    _____

Notes and Questions on the *Organization* of Reading 7

Part A: Paragraphs

Reading 7 tells the story of someone's trip. By now, you already know what basic *system of paragraphs* to expect. The following questions will guide you:

1. In which paragraph does the trip begin? What information comes before that point? What is the name of the paragraph leading to the main point?

2. In which paragraph does the trip end? How many paragraphs long is the body, then?

3. Is there a separate conclusion? There isn't, is there?

The system of paragraphs in Reading 7 is the same as in Reading 5. The end of the trip (in Reading 5, the end of the day) is the end of the composition. In other words, the last part of the *body* is the *conclusion*. This often happens when we write about a period of time.

Part B: Order

By now, you probably don't need questions to help you see when the *order of information* is *chronological*. Check the time words in Reading 7. Look again to see how the time is divided. In other words, where in the composition do you get the arrival and the departure? Where do you find information about the time in between? Now, go on to Model 7. See if it is organized the same way.

1

2

3

4

5

6

7

8

Model 7

A MEMORABLE TRIP

I took a wonderful trip with my family when I was ten years old. I remember it well. My aunt, uncle, and cousins lived on a little farm in the country outside Rome and they invited us to visit them. These cousins, Angelo and Gina, are the same cousins who live in Miami now. Our trip to visit them a long time ago was very different from our recent trip to Miami.

It was a Saturday morning when we left home. We got up early that morning before the sun rose. We were sleepy, but we were excited and ate breakfast quickly. We left home at 5:30 in order to get an early start. It took us three hours to get there in my father's old car. When we drove up to the house, my father honked the horn to announce our arrival. Everyone ran out to greet us. We all hugged and kissed each other.

We stayed for two days and had a wonderful time. We played outside all day and helped Uncle Vito feed the chickens. He taught us how to make wine. He also showed us how to play checkers. At night, Roberto and I played checkers with Angelo and Gina and listened to the grown-ups tell stories about their childhood.

When it was time to leave, we were very sad. My mother was especially sad to leave my Aunt Rosalina, her sister. They begged us to stay longer, but we had to leave. My father had to go to work the next day. As I look back, that trip was a long, long time ago. Aunt Rosalina and Uncle Vito are both dead; Gina and Angelo are living in Miami. The world is different now.

9

10

Composition 7

Instructions for Student's Composition

1. Write about a trip on 8½ × 11 loose-leaf notebook paper. Give details of the trip. Perhaps the trip was good; perhaps it was bad.

2. Write four paragraphs. Be sure to leave margins and indent for each paragraph. Put the following information in your paragraphs:

   Paragraph 1. Where did you go? When did you go? Why did you go?
   Paragraph 2. Tell about the beginning of the trip.
   Paragraph 3. How long did you stay? What did you do?
   Paragraph 4. Tell about coming home. Tell about your feelings.

3. Use as much of Model 7 as you need. Let it help you with grammar, vocabulary, ideas, and organization.

4. Your composition should look like this:

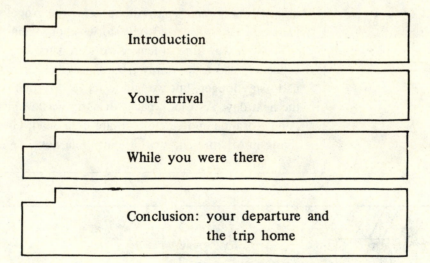

Introduction

Your arrival

While you were there

Conclusion: your departure and
the trip home

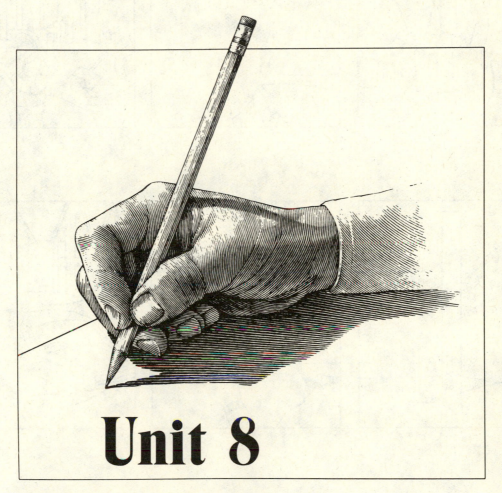

Unit 8

Composition Focus: Exposition

Organizational Focus: Classification

Grammatical Focus: Simple Present Tense

1

2

3

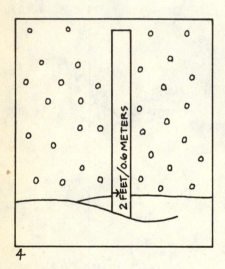

4

5

6

7

8

9

Reading 8

THE WEATHER IN CHICAGO

The weather is important to everyone. It is more than the subject of conversation. People's lives and moods change with the weather. My family and I once visited our friend, Salvatori, in Chicago in December. Never again! Oh, we will visit our friend again, but not in December. In that part of the United States, there are definitely four seasons: winter, spring, summer, and fall.

Winter is the unpleasant season. It snows a lot and people have trouble with their cars. When we were in Chicago, there were two feet of snow on the ground. Roberto and I built a snowman and threw snowballs at each other. That was fun, but Salvatori didn't have fun when his car got stuck in the snow. Sometimes, schools have to close because students can't get to school. People stay inside a lot and become depressed. When they go outside, they need to wear heavy coats, boots, hats, and gloves. It gets very, very cold. Our friend says that the temperature sometimes drops to 0° Fahrenheit and below! Brrr!

Spring and fall are lovely seasons there, according to Salvatori. Next time, we will visit him in the spring or fall. In the springtime, everything comes alive. The snow melts, the grass turns green, and flowers begin to bloom. People seem happy and spend more time outside. The sun shines almost every day. Salvatori says that the leaves turn orange, yellow, and red in the fall. The weather is still warm and pleasant. People drive to the country in order to see the fall colors. This is our friend's favorite season.

Summer is a good season in the north-central part of the United States, too. It gets hot and humid, Salvatori says, but there are fun things to do. He goes on picnics, swims a lot, and gives parties in his backyard. He relaxes and takes life easier. It sometimes rains there, he says, but that is not a problem. After the rain is over, the air is cool and pleasant.

People's lives certainly change with the weather. My life would be different in Chicago. I'm glad that I don't live there. Our friend, Salvatori, likes Chicago, but he isn't crazy about winter, either.

10

11

12

Exercise A: Simple Present Tense (3rd-Person Singular)

Please complete the following sentences. They tell about people in the summer and winter. Use the *simple present tense*. Begin each sentence with *In the* _____ *time, everyone* _____. Be careful with the 3rd-person singular verb form.

Part 1: Summertime in Chicago

  Example: go to the beach
        In the summertime, everyone goes to the beach.

1. go swimming

   I go swimming.
   _____ *He goes swimming.* _____

2. spend a lot of time outside

   _____

3. lie in the sun

   _____

4. go on picnics

   _____

5. have parties outside

   _____

6. relax

   _____

7. take life easy

   _____

8. sit in the yard

   _____

9. drive to the country

   _____

10. seem happy

_____

Part 2: Wintertime in Chicago

    Example: wear a heavy coat
                  In the wintertime, everyone wears a heavy coat.

173rd person

1. need boots and gloves

_____

2. have trouble driving

_____

3. stay inside a lot

_____

4. go skiing

_____

5. get sick

_____

6. sleep a lot

_____

7. play in the snow

_____

8. stay at home a lot

_____

9. throw snowballs

_____

10. have fun in the snow

_____

Exercise B: Expressions for Weather

Please rewrite each of the following sentences two times. Use *becomes* and *gets* in place of *is*. At the end of each sentence, use *in the (season)*. (Fill in the word that is best for your climate.) Every sentence says something about the *weather*.

DO
AFTER
109
oral

Example: It is warm.
            It becomes warm in the spring.
            It gets warm in the spring.

1. It is cool and pleasant.

   _____

   _____

2. It is hot and humid.

   _____

   _____

3. It is cold and rainy.

   _____

   _____

4. It is sunny.

   _____

   _____

5. It is hot and dry.

   _____

   _____

6. It is dark and cloudy.

   _____

   _____

7. It is cool and foggy.

_____

_____

Exercise C: Verbs for Weather

Please choose *verbs* from the following list to complete the sentences below. Use each verb only one time. The grammar and the meaning will help you decide. Every sentence says something about the **weather** and the *seasons* of the year in the northern part of the United States.

snows	turns	rains
gets	are	fall
drops	comes	shines
bloom		

1. In the springtime, the grass _____ green.

2. Flowers _____ in the spring.

3. The sun _____ almost every day in the summertime.

4. In the fall, leaves _____ from the trees.

5. In the spring, everything _____ alive.

6. In the winter, the temperature _____ to zero.

7. It sometimes _____ and we need to carry umbrellas.

8. It _____ very, very cold in the winter.

9. It _____ a lot in the winter and children like to throw snowballs.

10. There _____ four seasons: spring, summer, fall, and winter.

Exercise D: Word Order

Please rewrite the following sentences. Change the **word order**. Put the last part of each sentence first. Don't forget to use a comma after each part that you put first.

Do orally
pick out
prepositional
phrase &
move it

> *Example:* There are four seasons in the northern part of the United States.
> *In the northern part of the United States, there are four seasons.*

1. Everything comes alive in the springtime.

   _____

2. The sun shines almost every day in the summertime.

   _____

3. The leaves turn orange and red in the fall.

   _____

4. It gets hot and humid in the summer.

   _____

5. The air is cool and pleasant after the rain is over.

   _____

6. It snows a lot in the wintertime.

   _____

7. It gets very, very cold in the winter.

   _____

8. People need to wear heavy coats when they go outside.

   _____

9. There are different activities for each season.

   _____

10. There are four seasons in Chicago.

    _____

Notes and Questions on the *Organization* of Reading 8

Part A: Paragraphs

In Reading 8, the writer explains the weather in a certain region. In Chicago, where the writer's friend lives, there are four seasons. Therefore, you might expect six paragraphs: an introduction, one paragraph for each season, and a conclusion. However, there are only five paragraphs. The following questions will help you see the *system of paragraphs* in Reading 8:

1. Where does the writer introduce the topic? How does the writer introduce the topic?

2. Where does the writer explain each season? Does the writer combine any seasons in order to explain? If so, how?

3. Where does the writer end the explanation of the seasons? Is this the end of the body, then? What follows?

4. How does the writer conclude the composition? How does he begin the conclusion?

You can see that there are three basic parts in Reading 8: an *introduction* (the first paragraph), a *body* (the three following paragraphs), and a *conclusion* (the last paragraph). This is the usual *system of paragraphs* in composition writing. The paragraphs form the three basic parts. Be sure that you understand the system. Be sure that you understand how the paragraphs can form these parts and work together.

Part B: Order

The following questions will help you understand the *order of information* in Reading 8:

1. Does the writer explain the organization of the topic *weather*? How? Where?

2. How many subtopics, or classes, does the writer give you?

3. Does the writer give equal space to each subtopic?

4. Which season is explained first? Which ones follow? Is another order possible? Why does the writer talk about winter first?

In Unit 3, you learned about *classification*. It is a division into subtopics, or classes. *Weather* is a good topic to classify. Can you think of others? Now, go on to Model 8.

Model 8

THE WEATHER IN NEW ORLEANS

The weather! The weather! The weather! Don't people talk about anything else? It is true that the weather is important to us. Our activities and moods change with the weather. As the seasons change, our lives may become easy or difficult. My family and I live in New Orleans and New Orleans is different from some other parts of the United States. Here, we don't really have four seasons. We have summer, and then there is the rest of the year!

Summertime is a hot and humid time. The hot weather lasts from May to October. Many people turn on their air conditioners and stay indoors. The sun shines, except when it rains. It rains often, but it becomes hot and humid again right after the rain. People carry umbrellas for the rain and the sun! Summertime is also a fun time, especially for young people. My brother, Roberto, and I often go to the Gulf Coast to spend the day on the beach. We go with our friends. We take a picnic lunch and swim or lie in the sun. The beaches are especially crowded on the weekend. In the evening, we listen to music on the lakefront, go out to eat with our girlfriends or take them to a movie. Summer nights in New Orleans are warm and romantic. I love summer!

Fall, winter, and spring are really one big season. It rains a little, but it never snows. In December and January, the temperature is cool, but it rarely freezes. When it doesn't freeze, flowers bloom all

JANUARY	FEBRUARY	MARCH	APRIL
SAME THING!	SAME THING!	SAME THING!	ONE BIG SEASON!
MAY	JUNE	JULY	AUGUST
SEPTEMBER	OCTOBER	NOVEMBER	DECEMBER
		ONE BIG SEASON!	SAME THING!

8

9

year round. My mother loves that! She especially loves the month of April. That's when the azaleas and camellias bloom. Everyone in our family is very busy in fall, winter, and spring. My brother and I work part time and study full time. My parents work long hours.

The weather is important to all of us. Our lives change with the weather. Summer is the best season for me and my family. We can relax and take life a little easy. I don't like the busy, busy times. Why can't we have summer all year long?

10

11

12

Composition 8

Instructions for Student's Composition

1. Write a composition about the weather in a familiar place. Organize the weather into seasons. Describe the seasons. Write your composition on 8½ × 11 loose-leaf notebook paper.

2. Write four, five, or six paragraphs. The number of paragraphs depends on the number of seasons. You can combine seasons that are similar. Don't forget to indent for each paragraph and leave margins. Put the following information in your paragraphs:

   First paragraph. Introduce the topic. Is the weather important? Which part of the world are you writing about? How many seasons are there?

   Paragraphs 2, 3, (4, 5). Describe each season.

   Last paragraph. Conclude with general statements. What are your feelings?

3. Take what you need from Model 8. Let it help you with grammar, vocabulary, ideas, and organization.

4. Your composition should look like this:

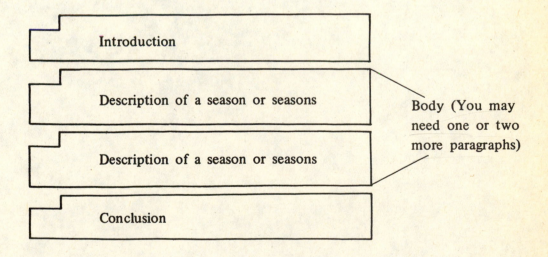

Unit 9

Composition Focus: Description

Organizational Focus: Classification
Balance of Contrasts

Grammatical Focus: Two-Word Verbs
Modals

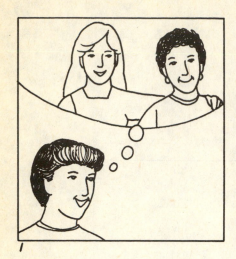

Reading 9

SYLVIA AND MARIA

Sylvia Gomez and Maria Herrera are very different. They look different and their personalities are different. Yet, they are cousins and roommates. They even date brothers. Maria is my girlfriend and Sylvia dates my bother, Roberto. Most people cannot believe that they are cousins. Some people cannot even believe that they are from the same country.

Sylvia is fairly tall with long blond hair. Maria is short and she has short brown hair. Sylvia is thin; Maria will tell you that she is fat, but she's really not. However, she is on a diet most of the time. Both of them are very pretty. Maria has sexy brown eyes and a nice smile. Her smile melts my heart. Sylvia's blue eyes are bright and beautiful. Most people think that Maria is Mexican or Italian; they say that Sylvia must be from Denmark or Sweden.

Their personalities are different, too. Both are very serious students, by Sylvia is quiet and Maria is not. Maria is not really loud, but she likes to go to parties and have fun. Maria is a social person. She likes to talk while Sylvia likes to listen. Maria likes to dance while Sylvia likes to watch people dance. Maria likes to turn on the TV and Sylvia likes to turn it off. Maria turns up the radio and Sylvia turns it down. Sylvia is very tidy and artistic. She loves

8

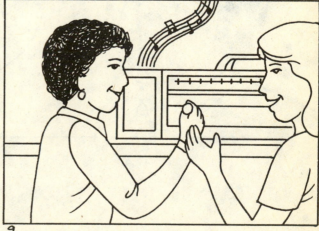

9

colors and well-organized space. Maria, on the other hand, is not especially tidy. She doesn't always put away her things or pick up her clothes. That upsets Sylvia. Yet, they both work hard to have a nice apartment.

Sylvia and Maria are very different, but both are nice people. Their differences make them very interesting. They are good friends and they love each other very much. Roberto and I love them, too.

10   11

12

Exercise A: Modals

Please rewrite the following sentences. Use the **modal auxiliaries** in parentheses. Put them into your sentences. Make any necessary changes.

> *Example:*   Most people *don't believe* that Maria and Sylvia are cousins.   (cannot)
> *Most people cannot believe that they are cousins.*

1. People *don't* believe that they are from the same country.   (cannot)

   _____

2. They think that Sylvia *is* from Denmark.   (might)

   _____

3. They say that Maria *is* Mexican or Italian.   (must)

   _____

4. Maria's smile *melts* your heart.   (will)

   _____

5. Maria *tells* you that she is fat.   (will)

   _____

6. Sylvia *relaxes* a little; she is too serious.   (should)

   _____

7. Because Sylvia is artistic, she *studies* art after she learns more English.   (may)

   _____

8. Maria is a little loud. She *quiets* down.   (should)

   _____

9. Sylvia and Maria *work* part time to earn money for food, rent, and tuition.   (must)

   _____

10. Sylvia and Maria *don't go* to a movie after school; they *go* to work. (can't)   (must)

   _____

Exercise B: Modals

Please "translate" the *meaning* of the **italicized** part of each sentence below. Choose the correct translation below each sentence.

1. Sylvia doesn't look Mexican. Some people think that she *might be* from Denmark. Others think that she *might be* from Sweden or Finland.

   a. probably is

   b. is possibly

   c. will be

2. Most people *cannot believe* that Maria and Sylvia are cousins.

   a. don't want to believe

   b. refuse to believe

   c. find it difficult to believe

3. Because Sylvia is artistic, she *may study* art after she finishes her English courses.

   a. will possibly study

   b. finds it easy to study

   c. has her parents' permission to study

4. Because Sylvia and Maria don't have much money, they *must work* to pay for the food, rent, and tuition.

   a. like to work

   b. enjoy working

   c. have to work

5. Maria is so short that she *can't reach* the top of the bookcase.

   a. is unable to reach

   b. doesn't want to reach

   c. isn't smart enough to reach

6. Sylvia is a little too serious; she *should relax* some.

   a. has to relax

   b. finds it possible to relax

   c. ought to relax

7. Maria and Sylvia *will visit* their families in Mexico City next summer.

   a. are thinking about visiting

   b. are going to visit

   c. are hoping to visit

8. After Maria and Sylvia visit their families, they *may spend* some time in Acapulco.

   a. are going to spend

   b. have to spend

   c. will possibly spend

9. Sylvia and Maria plan to cook dinner for Roberto and Bruno. The cupboard is bare. They *must go* shopping.

   a. find it absolutely necessary to go

   b. are thinking about going

   c. will possibly go

10. *Will* Maria and Sylvia *marry* Bruno and Roberto?

    a. Do _____ want to marry

    b. Are _____ going to marry

    c. Do _____ have their parents' permission to marry

Exercise C: Two-Word Verbs

Please rewrite each sentence or request below. Change the **noun object** to a **pronoun object**. Separate the **two parts of the verb** and put the pronoun object between.

Example: Please turn down the radio.
Please turn it down.

1. Would you please hand in your homework?

   _____

2. You should put away your notes before the examination.

   _____

3. Will you please turn up the TV?

   _____

4. Could you please fill out this form?

   _____

5. Throw away those old newspapers, please.

   _____

6. You must write down this telephone number.

   _____

7. Please pick up those pieces of paper.

   _____

8. You should look over these apples before you buy them.

   _____

9. You should turn on the news now if you want to watch it.

   _____

10. Please turn off that light when you finish studying.

   _____

Exercise D: Two-Word Verbs

Please rewrite the sentences below. Rewrite only the sentences that need *two-word verbs*. Take out the italicized part and put in a two-word verb. The italicized part gives the **meaning**. Choose from the list of two-word verbs below. Use each verb only one time.

pick up	*put away*	*turn off*
fill out	*hand in*	*turn up*
write down	*throw away*	*turn down*
look over	*turn on*	

Example: I need to *lower the volume on* the radio. The baby can't sleep.
I need to turn down the radio.

1. I should *give* my homework *to the teacher*. She expects to have it before we leave class.

    _____

2. You must *note* all the important information. You will need to have it in your notebook in order to study for the examination.

    _____

3. You may *dispose of* these old shoes. I don't need them any more. They are no good.

    _____

4. You should *raise the volume on* the radio. I can't hear it.

    _____

5. Will you please *complete* this application? We need your name, address, and social security number.

    _____

6. You should *examine* your answers. Look for careless mistakes.

    _____

7. Would you please *start* the TV. It's time for the news.

    _____

8. Please *remove* these pencils *from the floor*. Someone might fall.

_____

9. Please *stop* the radio. I can't sleep.

_____

10. Children should learn to *place* their toys *in the proper spot* after they finish playing.

_____

Notes and Questions on the *Organization* of Reading 9

Part A: Paragraphs

Reading 9 describes two people. There are four paragraphs. Look back at those paragraphs to identify the three basic parts: ***introduction, body,*** and ***conclusion***. The following questions will help you be sure:

1. Where does the writer introduce the topic? What is the topic?

2. Where does the main part begin? Where does it end? How long is it? How is it divided?

3. Where does the conclusion begin? How does the writer conclude the composition? What does the writer do with the topic in the conclusion?

Part B: Order

Look back at the introduction to the composition. Do you know what kind of order to expect in the body of the composition? Does the writer tell you? The following questions will help you be sure about the ***order of information*** in Reading 9:

1. The specific topic is *Sylvia and Maria*. What kind of topic is that? How can that kind of topic be organized? (Do you remember Unit 3?) Into how many subtopics does the writer divide the topic? What are the subtopics?

2. Which subtopic comes first in the body of the composition? Which comes second? Does it matter? It doesn't really, does it?

Do you remember that this kind of organization is called ***classification***? In Reading 9, there is something else happening within each class, or subtopic. Look closely. Do you see *blond–brown, tall–short, thin–fat* etc.? Notice that each characteristic is followed by the opposite characteristic. There is a balance. Let's call it a ***balance of contrasts***. Sometimes the contrasts are indirect. Pick out contrasts in the third paragraph. Then, go on to Model 9 to see the same techniques in operation.

1

2

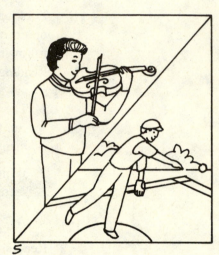

3

4

5

6

7

Model 9

ROBERTO AND I

My brother, Roberto, and I are different in many ways. We look different and our personalities are different. Of course, we are also similar in some ways, but the differences are probably more interesting.

I look like my mother's side of the family; Roberto looks more like my father's. He is fairly tall with light brown hair. I am short and my hair is dark brown, almost black. His eyes are green, while mine are dark brown to match my hair. Roberto has a medium build and he is more athletic. I am a little jealous of his muscles. I try to stay in shape, but I am a little heavy. My mother says that I eat too much. Yet, Roberto is the one who loves ice cream. Life is not fair!

Our personalities are different, too. I like music and can play the violin well. I can pick up a piece of music, look it over, and play it immediately. Everyone says that I have a lot of musical ability. Roberto, on the other hand, has athletic ability. He loves baseball and is an excellent pitcher. In college, he plans to major in physical education, while I plan to get a degree in music. In addition to our different abilities, I am more outgoing than Roberto. I love to be with people. Roberto isn't exactly shy, but he is a sensitive guy. He worries about our parents because they work so hard. He worries about our grandparents in Rome because they are old and Grandfather is ill. He also worries about his English. He is a little jealous of my English because mine is better. Yet, he is the big brother!

Our differences sometimes cause us problems. We sometimes argue and disagree. However, we love each other and accept our differences. We can't stay angry at each other for long; after all, we have to share a bedroom!

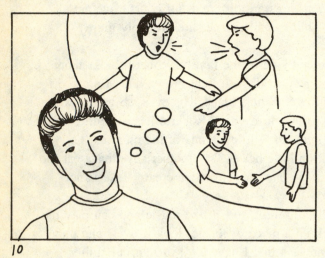

10

11

Composition 9

Instructions for Student's Composition

1. Write a composition about yourself and someone you know. Choose someone who is very different from you. Write about the differences. Always give your composition a title. Write your composition on 8½ × 11 loose-leaf notebook paper.

2. Write four paragraphs. Remember to indent and leave margins. Put the following information in your paragraphs:

    Paragraph 1. What are you writing about? Who are you writing about? Say that you are dividing the topic into *looks* and *actions*. What do people think?

    Paragraph 2. Describe the differences in physical appearance.

    Paragraph 3. Describe the differences in personality.

    Paragraph 4. Conclude with general statements. Do the differences cause problems? How do you feel about the differences?

3. Take what you need from Model 9. Let it help you with organization, grammar, ideas, and vocabulary.

4. Your composition should look like this:

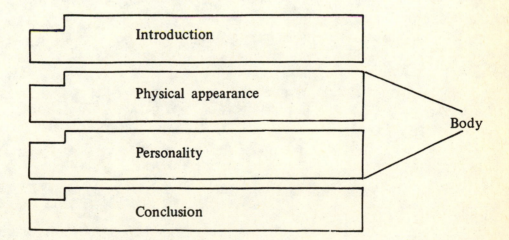

Unit 10

Composition Focus: Exposition

Organizational Focus: Classification

Grammatical Focus: Present Perfect Tense
                       Forms of Comparison

Reading 10

MY STAY IN NEW ORLEANS

My family and I arrived in the United States on March 4, 1985. We came here from Italy by plane. It was hard for us to leave our home and our relatives, but we wanted to make a new life here. Since that time, I have seen many new and interesting places. I have also learned a lot.

New Orleans was very strange to me in the beginning. It was very different from Rome, my hometown. New Orleans seemed small and uninteresting. I saw no grand buildings, wide boulevards, or ancient monuments. While some areas of town seemed clean and modern, others seemed old and dirty. Since then, I have become acquainted with New Orleans and I like it better. I have visited the New Orleans Museum of Art and the Audubon Zoo. I have taken a river cruise on the Delta Queen. I have taken a boat tour of the bayous and swamps. I have become familiar with the French Quarter and wonderful jazz music. I have eaten in wonderful restaurants. Now I know that New Orleans is as interesting as Rome. Now it seems as charming and friendly to me.

When I first arrived, I felt so lost and stupid. I didn't know any English at all. Since then, I have learned a lot of English. It has been difficult because Italian is very different from English. Italian grammar seems more regular and less idiomatic. Nevertheless, I

speak English almost like a native now. I have also learned a lot about American culture and the unique history of New Orleans. Last November, my family ate Thanksgiving turkey with some American families from our church. We have watched the fireworks over the Mississippi River on the Fourth of July. My brother, Roberto, and I have gone to some wonderful jazz concerts at Preservation Hall. We have seen the place where Andrew Jackson beat the British in the Battle of New Orleans. I still have a lot to learn, but I feel comfortable here now.

My family and I plan to stay in New Orleans forever. This is our new home. I hope to travel more in the future and visit all fifty states. I also hope to visit Italy soon to see my grandparents and all my old friends. I don't want them to forget me. I will never forget them.

Exercise A: Present Perfect Tense

Please answer the following question by completing the sentences below. Use the *present perfect tense* with *he has* + past participle.

    Question: What has Bruno seen, done, and learned since he arrived in the United States?

    Example: become acquainted with New Orleans
                     He has become acquainted with New Orleans.

1. visit the New Orleans Museum of Art

   _____

2. go to the Audubon Zoo

   _____

3. take a river cruise on the Delta Queen

   _____

4. take a boat tour of the swamps

   _____

5. become familiar with the French Quarter

   _____

6. eat in different restaurants

   _____

7. learn about jazz music

   _____

8. learn a lot of English

   _____

9. share a Thanksgiving turkey with some American families

   _____

10. learn a lot about American culture

   _____

11. watch fireworks over the Mississippi River

_____

12. go to some jazz concerts

_____

13. see the place where Andrew Jackson fought the Battle of New Orleans

_____

14. make plans to visit all fifty states

_____

15. become comfortable here

_____

Exercise B: Expressions of Comparison

Compare New York City and Rome, Italy. Use the following information to make your statements of comparison.

Example: New York—Rome   (different)
New York is different from Rome.

1. New York—Rome   (dirtier)

_____

2. New York—Rome   (noisier)

_____

3. New York—Rome   (more modern)

_____

4. New York—Rome   (more interesting)

_____

5. New York—Rome   (more commercial)

_____

6. New York—Rome   (larger)

_____

7. Rome—New York   (older)

_____

8. Rome—New York   (more beautiful)

_____

9. Rome—New York   (more historical)

_____

10. Rome—New York   (more familiar to Bruno)

_____

Exercise C: Cohesion (Reference)

The italicized part of each sentence below refers the reader to another point of information in Reading 10. Check Reading 10 for each point. Please circle the letter *a, b,* or *c,* to show the correct reference.

1. *We* came here from Italy by plane.
   Who does *we* refer to?

   a. Bruno

   b. the relatives

   c. Bruno and his family

2. Since *that time*, I have seen many new and interesting places.
   What does *that time* refer to?

   a. coming to the USA by plane

   b. saying good-bye

   c. leaving Italy and coming to the United States

3. *It* was very different from Rome, my hometown.
   What does *it* refer to?

   a. New Orleans

   b. Italy

   c. the United States

4. While some areas of town seemed clean and modern, *others* seemed old and dirty.
   What does *others* refer to?

   a. other areas of Rome

   b. other areas of New Orleans

   c. other areas of the United States

5. *It* has been difficult because Italian is very different from English.
   What does *it* refer to?

   a. Italian grammar

   b. learning English

   c. idioms

6. Italian grammar seems *more* regular and *less* idiomatic.
   What is understood? *More regular* than what? *Less idiomatic* than what?

   a. than English grammar

   b. than American culture

   c. than the history of New Orleans

7. I speak English almost *like a native* now.
   What is understood? *Like a native* does what?

   a. speaks English

   b. speaks Italian

   c. uses Italian grammar

8. This is *our* new home.
   Who does *our* refer to?

   a. Mr. and Mrs. Baroni's

   b. Bruno and his family's

   c. Bruno and Roberto's

9. I *also* hope to visit Italy soon.
   What does *also* include?

   a. visiting all fifty states

   b. seeing my old friends

   c. visiting New Orleans

10. I don't want *them* to forget me.
    Who does *them* refer to?

    a. my parents

    b. all fifty states

    c. my grandparents and all my old friends

Exercise D: Cohesion (Connection)

Please complete the following sentences. Choose *a, b,* or *c.*

1. Bruno arrived in the United States on March 4, 1985. _____, he has seen and done a lot.

    a. Then

    b. Since then

    c. After that

2. _____, New Orleans was very strange to him. Now he feels comfortable in the city.

    a. At first

    b. Afterwards

    c. Finally

3. _____ some areas of New Orleans seemed clean and modern to Bruno, others seemed old and dirty.

    a. On the other hand

    b. Because

    c. While

4. In the beginning, New Orleans seemed small and uninteresting to Bruno. _____ it seems friendly and charming.

    a. Then

    b. Later

    c. Now

5. _____ Bruno first arrived, he felt so lost and stupid.

    a. While

    b. When

    c. Where

6. English was difficult for Bruno to learn. _____, he speaks well now.

    a. Nevertheless

    b. At that point

    c. Because

7. Bruno has learned a lot of English. He has _____ learned a lot about American culture.

   a. if

   b. also

   c. but

8. Bruno has seen the place _____ Jackson fought the Battle of New Orleans.

   a. why

   b. when

   c. where

9. Bruno still has a lot to learn, _____ he feels comfortable here now.

   a. but

   b. and

   c. so

10. _____ Bruno wants to see more places in the United States, he is planning a trip across the country.

   a. After

   b. Before

   c. Because

Notes and Questions on the *Organization* of Reading 10

Part A: Paragraphs

Reading 10 tells the story of Bruno's stay in the United States. There are four paragraphs. Look back at those paragraphs. Identify the three basic parts within the *system of paragraphs*: *introduction, body,* and *conclusion.* Tell why you think so.

Part B: Order

The title of Reading 10 suggests a period of time. There is an important date in the introduction. You might, therefore, expect the *order of information* to be chronological. However, it is not. The following questions will help you decide what it is:

1. What does the writer say about the time since his arrival? How is it divided in the introduction? What are the subtopics?

2. Which subtopic does the writer discuss first? How does the writer get into that subtopic?

3. Which subtopic is next? How many examples does the writer give within that subtopic?

4. How does the writer conclude the discussion of the subtopics? Does the writer add new information?

Reading 10 uses *classification* as a tool to organize the information. The writer organizes the contents of time. *Contrasts* help to show change and progression within the period of time.

Take a moment to review all the different ways to order information. Then, go on to Model 10.

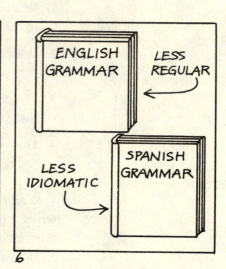

Model 10

LIFE IN NEW ORLEANS

August 1, 1986, was an important day! On that day, I arrived in the United States. I traveled to New Orleans from Mexico by plane. I came with my cousin, Sylvia. We were so scared! We didn't know anyone in New Orleans and we had no place to live. Since that time, I have seen and done a lot. I have also learned many new things.

At first, I didn't like New Orleans. It was very different from Mexico City, my hometown. It seemed quieter and less interesting. I felt homesick for the excitement of Mexico City. Since then, I have become acquainted with New Orleans and I like it much better. I have discovered Tipitina's, Snug Harbor, and the Maple Leaf where local musicians play. I really like the music of the Neville Brothers. I don't have a lot of time for fun, but my boyfriend, Bruno, and I enjoy these places on the weekend. I have visited Lafayette and other Louisiana towns where people still speak French and keep their old ways. I love all the interesting accents. Now I think that New Orleans and the area around it are almost as exciting as Mexico City.

When I arrived, I already knew a lot of English, but I still needed some practice. Since then, I have become very fluent and my accent is much better. It hasn't been easy because English is a difficult language. It seems less regular and more idiomatic than Spanish. Nevertheless, I am proud of my English now. I have also learned a lot about American culture. Each person seems to have more freedom, but each person has more responsibility, too. I have never been so free and worked so hard! I have met many American students and talked to them. One American friend invites me to her house often. Last December, I celebrated Christmas with her family. Sylvia went, too. I am beginning to feel at home in New Orleans now.

I plan to stay in New Orleans until I graduate from college.
Then, I plan to go back to Mexico City. What about my boyfriend,
Bruno? I don't know. We haven't really talked about the future.
Now I am enjoying the present.

Composition 10

Instructions for Student's Composition

1. Write a composition about your stay in the United States or your life in the city where you live. Divide you composition into two parts: what you have seen/done and what you have learned. Give your composition a title. Write on 8½ × 11 paper.

2. Write four paragraphs. Remember to indent and leave margins. Put the following information in your paragraphs:

   Paragraph 1. When did you arrive? How did you come and where did you come from? Show that you are dividing the topic into two parts: *seen/done* and *learned*.

   Paragraph 2. Describe the beginning. What was different between the old place and the new place? What have you seen/done in the new place?

   Paragraph 3. What have you learned in the new place?

   Paragraph 4. Conclude with your future plans.

3. Use Model 10. Let it help you with grammar, ideas, vocabulary, and organization.

4. Your composition should look like this:

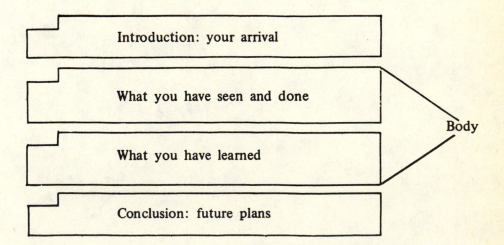

Introduction: your arrival

What you have seen and done

What you have learned

Body

Conclusion: future plans